Fodor's P O C K E T 2001

S0-AXJ-277

madrid

Excerpted from *Fodor's Spain 2001*

fodor's travel publications
new york · toronto · london · sydney · auckland

www.fodors.com

contents

maps and plans

ON THE ROAD WITH FODOR'S

EVERY TRIP IS A SIGNIFICANT TRIP. Acutely aware of that fact, we've pulled out all stops in preparing Fodor's Pocket Madrid 2001. To guide you in putting together your Madrid experience, we've created multiday itineraries and regional tours. And to direct you to the places that are truly worth your time and money, we've found an endearingly picky know-it-all we're pleased to call our writer. Having seen all corners of Madrid, he's a real expert. If you knew him, you'd poll him for tips yourself.

Raised in Cornwall, England, journalist **Edward Owen** has worked in London, Toronto, and Sydney, and, since 1980, Madrid. Long a foreign correspondent for London's Times, Sunday Times, and Daily Express, he now specializes in travel, wine, and gastronomy. Ed extols the Spanish climate and the Spaniards' vim and vigor, and makes the most of the country's tremendous variety.

Don't Forget to Write

Keeping a travel guide fresh and up-to-date is a big job. So we love your feedback—positive and negative—and follow up on all suggestions. Contact the Pocket Madrid editor at editors@fodors.com or c/o Fodor's, 280 Park Avenue, New York, New York 10017. And have a wonderful trip!

Karen Cure
Editorial Director

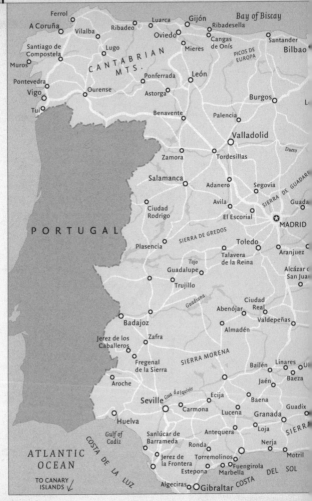

Bay of Biscay

Ferrol
Luarca
Gijón
A Coruña
Vilalba
Ribadeo
Ribadesella
Oviedo
Santiago de
Compostela
Lugo
Mieres
Cangas
de Onís
Santander
Bilbao
Muros
CANTABRIAN
PICOS DE
EUROPA
MTS.
Ponferrada
León
Pontevedra
Astorga
Burgos
Vigo
Ourense
L
Tui
Benavente
Palencia
Valladolid
Zamora
Tordesillas
Duero
Salamanca
Adanero
Segovia
SIERRA DE GUADARR
Avila
Guada
Ciudad
Rodrigo
El Escorial
MADRID
PORTUGAL
SIERRA DE GREDOS
Toledo
Plasencia
Talavera
de la Reina
Aranjuez
Tajo
Guadalupe
Alcázar d
San Juar
Trujillo
Guadiana
Ciudad
Real
Abenójar
Badajoz
Valdepeñas
Zafra
Almadén
Jerez de los
Caballeros
Fregenal
de la Sierra
SIERRA MORENA
Bailén
Linares
U
Aroche
Jaén
Baeza
Seville
Gua dalquivir
Ecija
Baena
Guadix
Huelva
Carmona
Lucena
Granada
Gulf of
Cadiz
Sanlúcar de
Barrameda
Antequera
Loja
SIERRA
Nerja
ATLANTIC
OCEAN
Ronda
Torremolinos
Motril
Jerez de
la Frontera
Fuengirola
DEL SOL
COSTA DE LA LUZ
Estepona
Marbella
COSTA
TO CANARY
ISLANDS
Algeciras
Gibraltar

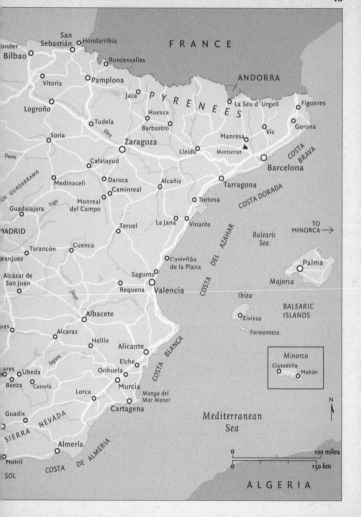

madrid

In This Section

introducing madrid

LIFE IN MADRID is lived in crowded streets and noisy cafés, where talking, toasting, and tapa-tasting last long into the night. The capital's endless energy is hard to resist, and its sociable style invites you to jump right in.

Madrid's other main attraction is its unsurpassed collection of art by some of the world's great masters, among them Goya, El Greco, Velázquez, Picasso, and Dalí. Nowhere else will you find such a concentration of masterpieces as in the three museums—the Prado, the Reina Sofía, and the Thyssen-Bornemisza—that make up Madrid's so-called Paseo del Arte (Art Walk).

The first thing you notice here may be the bright blue sky, as immortalized in the paintings of Velázquez. Despite 20th-century pollution, the heavens are still in evidence thanks to breezes that sweep down from the Guadarrama mountains, blowing away urban smog. The skyline has its share of skyscrapers, but these are far outnumbered by more typically *madrileño* towers of red brick crowned by gray slate roofs and spires. Built in the 16th and 17th centuries by the Habsburgs, who made Madrid the capital of the Iberian realm, this architecture gives parts of Madrid a timeless, Old World look. Monumental neoclassical structures, like the Prado Museum, the Royal Palace, and the Puerta de Alcalá arch—the sights most often seen by travelers—make up Madrid's other historic face. Most of these were built in the 18th century, during the reign of Bourbon monarch Charles III; inspired by the enlightened ideas of the age, Charles also created the Parque del Retiro and the broad, leafy boulevard Paseo del Prado.

Modern-day Madrid sprawls northward in block after block of dreary, high-rise brick apartment and office buildings. The population of three million is also moving into surrounding villages and new suburbs, creating traffic problems in and around the city. These new quarters and many of Madrid's crumbling old residential neighborhoods may seem unprepossessing, but don't be put off by first impressions. Much of the city's appeal comes from its vivacious people and the electricity they generate, whether at play in bars and clubs or at work in Spain's finance, advertising, television, and film industries, all headquartered here.

Poised on a plateau 2,120 ft above sea level, Madrid is the highest capital in Europe. It can thus be one of the world's hottest cities in summer, and freezing cold in winter. Spring and summer are the best times to visit, when balmy evenings have everyone in town lingering at outdoor cafés; but each season has its own charms. In winter, steamy café windows and all-night street festivals beckon, and the blue skies are particularly crisp and bright—and that's when Madrid is, according to a local bumper sticker, the next best place to heaven.

QUICK TOURS

TOUR ONE

If you have only a day or two, limit yourself to a couple museums and devote the rest of your time to wandering. See the works of Spain's great masters at the **Museo del Prado**; then visit the **Palacio Real** for a regal display of art, architecture, and history. The palace tour includes admission to the Royal Library and Royal Armory, both sights in their own right. Stroll from Paseo de la Castellana to Paseo del Prado to see the fountains at **Plaza**

Colón: Fuente de la Cibeles and **Fuente de Neptuno.** Behold the **Puerta del Sol,** then relax at an outdoor café on the **Plaza Mayor.** Finally, pop into some of the historic tapas bars along **Cava de San Miguel.**

TOUR TWO

With three or four days you can uncover historic Madrid, visit more museums, and make an excursion outside the city. Follow the two-day plan above; then visit the **Centro de Arte Reina Sofía** and the **Museo Thyssen-Bornemisza.** Try not to miss the 16th-century **Convento de las Descalzas Reales.** Explore the Mudéjar architecture and flamboyant plateresque decoration of medieval Madrid in the **Plaza de la Villa** and around the **Plaza de la Paja.** Venture outside the capital to spend your fourth day at **El Escorial,** a grand monastery, or **Chinchón,** a true Castillian village.

FESTIVALS AND SEASONAL EVENTS

➤ DECEMBER: **New Year's Eve** ticks away at the Puerta del Sol, where crowds gather to eat one grape on each stroke of midnight.

➤ JANUARY: **Epiphany** (Jan. 6) is a Spanish child's Christmas: youngsters leave their shoes on the doorstep to be filled with gifts from the Three Kings. In many towns the Wise Men arrive the night of January 5 by boat, camel, or car and are featured in parades.

➤ MAY: **San Isídro** (May 15) kicks off two weeks of the best bullfighting in Spain.

➤ JUNE: **Corpus Christi** (June 14) is celebrated with processions.

In This Section

here and there

MADRID IS A COMPACT CITY with a rich urban texture. Broad *avenidas*, twisting medieval alleys, stately gardens, and tiny taverns are all jumbled together in areas easily covered on foot. Indeed, walking is the best way to experience those special moments whose images linger—peeking in on a guitar maker at work, or watching a child dip sweet *churros* (deep-fried batter twists, a classic Madrileño snack) into a steamy cup of hot chocolate.

Most of the major sights are concentrated in a downtown area 2½ km (1½ mi) across, stretching between the Royal Palace and the Parque del Retiro. Madrid's three world-class art museums—the Prado, the Reina Sofía, and the Thyssen-Bornemisza—are all within 1 km (½ mi) of each other along the leafy Paseo del Prado, sometimes called the Paseo del Arte.

Sadly, muggings are a serious problem in Madrid, and tourists are frequent targets. Be on your guard as you wander, and make an effort to blend in: wear dark clothes, try to keep cameras concealed, and avoid flamboyant map reading. The Japanese Embassy has complained to Madrid authorities that tourists who appear East Asian seem to be at particular risk.

Numbers in the text correspond to numbers in the margin and on the Madrid Exploring map.

CENTRAL MADRID

Between the Royal Palace and the Puerta del Sol is a stretch of about 1 km (½ mi) that's loaded with historic sites.

A Good Walk

Begin at the **Puerta del Sol** ①, the center of Madrid. If you stand with your back to the clock, Calle Arenal leaves the plaza from the far left: walk down Arenal and turn right into Plaza Celenque. Up on your left at the corner with Calle Misericordia is the **Convento de las Descalzas Reales** ②. Follow Misericordia and turn left into the charming Plaza de San Martín to return to Calle Arenal. Turn right and walk down to Plaza San Isabel II; then, crossing the plaza to your right, walk to the end of the short Calle Arrieta, at which point you'll face the **Convento de la Encarnación** ③. Turn left here into Calle San Quintin and you'll enter the semicircular **Plaza de Oriente** ④. Walk to the right (north) down Calle Bailén.

Here you have a choice of going directly to the magnificent **Palacio Real** ⑤, on your left, or visiting its gardens (1 km/½ mi farther on) and/or taking a cable-car ride. For the latter, cross Calle Bailén and walk to the right: you'll have a lovely view across the formal **Jardines Sabatini** ⑥ over to the Casa de Campo park and the distant Guadarrama Mountains. Walk up Bailén, avoiding the overpass, and turn left down Cuesta de San Vicente, then left into Paseo Virgin del Puerto for the entrance to the palace gardens and the **Campo del Moro** ⑦. If you go straight, crossing the overpass, you'll reach Calle Ferraz; follow the Parque del Oeste on the left and you'll reach the Egyptian **Templo de Debod** ⑧. Farther along Paseo de Pintor Rosales, in the park, is the **Teléferico** ⑨ cable car to the Casa de Campo, which grants panoramic views of Madrid.

Opposite the Royal Palace on the plaza is Madrid's opera house, the **Teatro Real** ⑩. To its right is the Cafe Oriente, a good pit stop. Walking down Bailén with the palace on your right, you can enter its huge courtyard and admire the view from the top of the escarpment. Alongside the palace is the **Catédral de la Almudena** ⑪. Walk past the cathedral and turn right onto Calle

Mayor: on your left, in Cuesta de la Vega, are the remains of Madrid's **Arab Wall** ⑫, next to the Parque Emir Mohammed I.

Walk back east up Calle Mayor, crossing Bailén. Turn left into Calle San Nicolás to see the church of **San Nicolás de las Servitas** ⑬. Return to Mayor and press ahead: on your right you'll see the **Plaza de la Villa** ⑭, with Madrid's city hall on the right. Farther up Mayor, bear right in Plaza Morenas and enter the **Plaza Mayor** ⑮ through the arch. The Andalusian Torre de Oro bar on the left displays gory pictures of bullfights, not for the squeamish. On the far side, at No. 33, is the restaurant El Soportal, which gives the plaza's best free tapas with each drink order. (Beware of prices at the other restaurants, especially if you sit outside.) Exit the plaza to the left of El Soportal and head down Calle de Postas and back to the Puerta del Sol. Proceed up the right side of Sol, past the headquarters of the regional government, and perhaps take a tapa in the charming old shop at the restaurant Lhardy, on Carrera de San Jerónimo.

TIMING

Without side trips to the palace gardens or the cable car, you can cover this walk in two hours. Set aside an additional morning or afternoon to visit the Royal Palace.

Sights to See

⑫ **ARAB WALL.** The city of Madrid was founded on Calle Cuesta de la Vega at the ruins of this wall, which protected a fortress built here in the 8th century by Emir Mohammed I. In addition to being an excellent defensive position, the site had plentiful water and was called Mayrit, which is Arabic for "water source" and the likely origin of the city's name. All that remains of the *medina*—the old Arab city that formed within the walls of the fortress—is the neighborhood's crazy quilt of streets and plazas, which probably follow the same layout they followed more than 1,100 years ago. The park **Emir Mohammed I,** alongside the wall, hosts concerts and plays in the summer.

exploring madrid

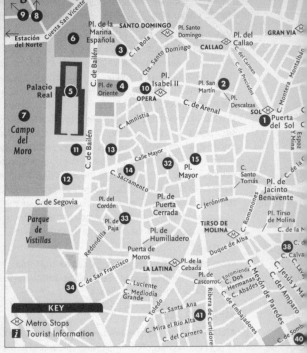

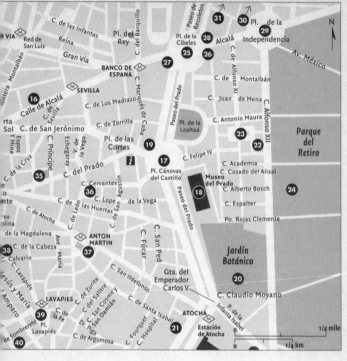

❼ CAMPO DEL MORO (Moors' Field). Below the Sabatini Gardens, but accessible only by an entrance on the far side, is the Campo del Moro. Clusters of shady trees, winding paths, and a long lawn leading up to the Royal Palace make for strategically beautiful photographs. Even without considering the riches inside, the palace's immense size (it's twice as large as Buckingham Palace) inspires awe.

⓫ CATÉDRAL DE LA ALMUDENA. The first stone of the cathedral (which adjoins the Royal Palace to the south) was laid in 1883 by King Alfonso XII, and the end result was consecrated by Pope John Paul II in 1993. The building was intended to be Gothic in style, with needles and spires, but as time ran long and money ran short, the design was simplified by Fernando Chueca Goltia into the more austere classical form you see today. The cathedral houses the remains of Madrid's patron saint, San Isidro (St. Isidore), and a wooden statue of Madrid's female patron saint, the Virgin of Almudena, which is said to have been discovered following the Christian reconquest of Madrid in 1085. Legend has it that a divinely inspired woman named María led authorities to a secret spot in the old wall of the Alcázar (which in Arabic can also be called *almudeyna*), where the statue was found framed by two lighted candles inside a grain storage vault. That wall is part of the cathedral's foundation. *C. Bailén s/n, tel. 91/548–9900. Free. Daily 10–1:30 and 6–7:45.*

❸ CONVENTO DE LA ENCARNACIÓN (Convent of the Incarnation). Once connected to the Royal Palace by an underground passageway, this Augustinian convent was founded in 1611 by the wife of Felipe III. It holds several artistic treasures, but its biggest attraction is its reliquary, which holds among the sacred bones a vial containing the dried blood of St. Pantaleón, which is said to liquefy every year on July 27. You can enter Encarnación on the same ticket as the Convent of Descalzas Reales (☞ *below*). *Plaza de la Encarnación 1, tel. 91/547–0510. 400 ptas. Wed. and Sat. 10:30–2:30 and 4–5:30, Sun. 11–2.*

② **CONVENTO DE LAS DESCALZAS REALES** (Convent of the Royal Barefoot Nuns). This 16th-century building was restricted for 200 years to women of royal blood. Its plain, brick-and-stone facade hides a treasure trove, including paintings by Zurbarán, Titian, and Brueghel the Elder, as well as a hall of sumptuous tapestries crafted from drawings by Peter Paul Rubens. The convent was founded in 1559 by Juana of Austria, whose daughter shut herself up here rather than endure marriage to Felipe II. A handful of nuns (not necessarily royal) still live here, cultivating their own vegetables in the convent's garden. You must visit as part of a guided tour, usually conducted once a day in English and the rest of the day in Spanish. *Plaza de las Descalzas Reales 3, tel. 91/542–0059. 700 ptas. Tues.–Thurs. and Sat. 10:30–12:45 and 4–5:45, Fri. 10:30–12:45, Sun. 11–1:45.*

⑥ **JARDINES SABATINI** (Sabatini Gardens). The formal gardens to the north of the Royal Palace are crawling with stray cats, but they're a pleasant place to rest or watch the sun set.

★ **⑤** **PALACIO REAL.** The Royal Palace was commissioned in the early 18th century by the first of Spain's Bourbon rulers, Felipe V, on the same strategic site where Madrid's first Alcázar (Moorish fortress) was built in the 9th century.

Before you enter, stroll around the graceful **Patio de Armas** and admire the classical French architecture. King Felipe was obviously inspired by his childhood days at Versailles with his grandfather Louis XIV. Look for the stone statues of Inca prince Atahualpa and Aztec king Montezuma, perhaps the only tributes in Spain to these pre-Columbian American rulers. Notice how the steep bluff drops westward to the Manzanares River—on a clear day, this vantage point also commands a good view of the mountain passes leading into Madrid from Old Castile, and it becomes obvious why the Moors picked this particular spot for a fortress.

Inside, the palace's 2,800 rooms compete with each other for over-the-top opulence. A nearly two-hour guided tour in English winds a mile-long path through the palace. Highlights include the **Salón de Gasparini,** King Carlos III's private apartments—a riot of rococo decoration, with swirling, inlaid floors and curlicued, ceramic wall and ceiling decoration, all glistening in the light of a 2-ton crystal chandelier; the **Salón del Trono,** an exceedingly grand throne room with the royal seats of King Juan Carlos and Queen Sofía; and the **banquet hall,** the palace's largest room, which seats up to 140 people for state dinners. No monarch has lived here since 1931, when Alfonso XIII was hounded out of the country by a populace fed up with centuries of royal oppression. The current king and queen live in the far simpler Zarzuela Palace on the outskirts of Madrid, using this palace only for state functions and official occasions such as the first Middle East peace talks, held here in 1991.

You can also visit the **Biblioteca Real** (Royal Library), which has a first edition of Cervantes's *Don Quijote*; the **Museo de Música** (Music Museum), where five stringed instruments by Stradivarius form the world's largest collection; the **Armería Real** (Royal Armory), with its vast array of historic suits of armor and some frightening medieval torture implements; and the **Real Oficina de Farmacía** (Royal Pharmacy), with an assortment of vials and flasks that were used to mix the king's medicines. *C. Bailén s/n, tel. 91/542–0059. 950 ptas., guided tour 1,000 ptas. Tues.–Sat. 9–6 (Oct.–Mar. 9–5), Sun. 9–3 (Oct.–Mar. 9–2). Closed during official receptions.*

❹ PLAZA DE ORIENTE. The stately plaza in front of the Royal Palace is surrounded by massive stone statues of various Spanish monarchs from Ataulfo to Fernando VI. These sculptures were meant to be mounted on the railing on top of the palace (where there are now stone urns), but Queen Isabel of Farnesio, one of the first royals to live in the palace, had them removed because she was afraid their enormous weight would bring the roof down.

Well, that's what she *said* . . . according to palace insiders, the queen wanted the statues removed because her own likeness had not been placed front and center.

The statue of **King Felipe IV** in the center of the plaza was the first equestrian bronze ever cast with a rearing horse. The action pose comes from a Velázquez painting of the king with which the monarch was so smitten that in 1641 he commissioned an Italian artist, Pietro de Tacca, to turn it into a sculpture. De Tacca enlisted Galileo's help in configuring the statue's weight so that it wouldn't topple over.

In the minds of most Madrileños, the Plaza de Oriente is forever linked with Francisco Franco. The *generalísimo* liked to speak from the roof of the Royal Palace to his thousands of followers as they crammed into the plaza below. Even now, on the November anniversary of Franco's death, the plaza fills with supporters, most of whom are old-timers, though in a few recent years the occasion has drawn swastika-waving skinheads from other European countries in a chilling fascist tribute.

⑭ PLAZA DE LA VILLA. Madrid's town council has met in this medieval-looking complex since the Middle Ages, and it's now the city hall. Just two blocks west of the Plaza Mayor on Calle Mayor, it was once called Plaza de San Salvador for a church that used to stand here. The oldest building is the **Casa de los Lujanes,** on the east side—it's the one with the Mudéjar tower. Built as a private home in the late 15th century, the house carries the Lujanes crest over the main doorway. Also on the plaza's east end is the brick-and-stone **Casa de la Villa,** built in 1629, a classic example of Madrid design with its clean lines and spire-topped corner towers. Connected by an overhead walkway, the **Casa de Cisneros** was commissioned in 1537 by the nephew of Cardinal Cisneros. It's one of Madrid's rare examples of the flamboyant plateresque style, which has been likened to splashing water—a liquid exuberance wrought in stone. *C. Mayor. Guided tour in Spanish Mon. at 5.*

⑮ PLAZA MAYOR. Austere, grand, and often surprisingly quiet compared to the rest of Madrid, this arcaded square has seen it all: autos-da-fé (trials of faith, i.e., public burnings of heretics); the canonization of saints; criminal executions; royal marriages, such as that of Princess María and the King of Hungary in 1629; bullfights (until 1847); masked balls; fireworks; and all manner of events and celebrations. It still hosts fairs, bazaars, and performances.

Measuring 360 ft by 300 ft, Madrid's Plaza Mayor is one of the largest and grandest public squares in Europe. It was designed by Juan de Herrera, the architect to Felipe II and designer of the El Escorial monastery, northwest of Madrid. Construction of the plaza lasted just two years and was finished in 1620 under Felipe III, whose equestrian statue stands in the center. The inauguration ceremonies included the canonization of four Spanish saints: Teresa of Ávila, Ignatius of Loyola, Isidro (Madrid's male patron saint), and Francis Xavier.

This space was once occupied by a city market, and many of the surrounding streets retain the names of the trades and foodstuffs once headquartered there. Nearby are Calle de Cuchilleros (Knifemakers' Street), Calle de Lechuga (Lettuce Street), Calle de Fresa (Strawberry Street), and Calle de Botoneros (Buttonmakers' Street). The plaza's oldest building is the one with the brightly painted murals and the gray spires, called Casa de la Panadería (the Bakery) in honor of the bread shop on top of which it was built. Opposite is the Casa de la Carnicería (the Butcher Shop), now a police station.

The plaza is closed to motorized traffic, making it a pleasant place to sit in the sun or while away a warm summer evening at one of the sidewalk cafés, watching alfresco artists, street musicians, and Madrileños from all walks of life. Sunday morning brings a stamp and coin market. Around Christmas the plaza fills with stalls selling trees, ornaments, and nativity scenes, as well as all types of practical jokes and tricks for

December 28, *Día de los Inocentes*—a Spanish version of April Fool's Day.

❶ PUERTA DEL SOL. Always crowded with both people and exhaust fumes, Sol is the nerve center of Madrid's traffic. The city's main subway interchange is below, and buses fan out through the city from here. A brass plaque in the sidewalk on the south side of the plaza marks Kilometer 0, the spot from which all distances in Spain are measured. The restored 1756 French-neoclassical building near the marker now houses the offices of the regional government, but during Franco's reign it was the headquarters of his secret police, and it's still known folklorically as the Casa de los Gritos (House of Screams). Across the square is a bronze statue of Madrid's official symbol, a bear with a *madroño* (strawberry tree), and a statue of King-Mayor Carlos III on horseback.

❸ SAN NICOLÁS DE LAS SERVITAS (Church of St. Nicholas of the Servitas). This church tower is one of the oldest buildings in Madrid, and there is some debate over whether it once formed part of an Arab mosque. It was more likely built after the Christian reconquest of Madrid in 1085, but the brickwork and the horseshoe arches are clear evidence that it was crafted by either Moorish workers (Mudéjars) or Spaniards well versed in the style. Inside the church, exhibits detail the Islamic history of early Madrid. *Near the Plaza de San Nicolás, tel. 91/559–4064. Donation suggested. Tues.– Sun. 6:30 AM–8:30 PM or by appointment.*

❿ TEATRO REAL (Royal Theater). This neoclassical theater was built in 1850 and was long a cultural center for Madrileño society. Plagued by disasters more recently, including fires, a bombing, and profound structural problems, the house went dark in 1988. Closed for almost a decade for indulgent restoration, it reopened to worldwide fanfare in 1997. Now replete with golden balconies, plush seats, and state-of-the-art stage equipment for operas and ballets, the theater is a modern showpiece with its vintage appeal intact. *Plaza de Isabel II, tel. 91/516–0600.*

⑨ TELEFÉRICO (cable car). Kids love this cable car, which takes you from just above the Rosaleda gardens in the Parque del Oeste to the center of Casa de Campo. Be warned, however, that the walk from where the cable car drops you off to the zoo and the amusement park is at least 2 km (1 mi), and you'll have to ask directions. *Estación Terminal Teleférico, Jardines Rosaleda (at C. Marques de Urquijo), tel. 91/541–7450. 535 ptas. Apr.–Sept., daily noon–sundown; Oct.–Mar., weekends noon–3 and 4–6.*

⑧ TEMPLO DE DEBOD. This authentic 4th-century BC Egyptian temple was donated to Spain in gratitude for its technical assistance with the construction of the Aswan Dam. It's near the site of the former Montaña barracks, where Madrileños bloodily crushed the beginnings of a Francoist uprising in 1936. *Hill in Parque de la Montaña, near Estación del Norte, tel. 91/765–1008. 300 ptas.; free Wed. and Sun. Tues.–Fri. 10–1:30 and 4:30–6 (Apr.–Sept. 4:30–7:45), weekends 10–1:30.*

THE ART WALK

Madrid's star cultural attractions are its three superlative art museums, all within walking distance of each other via the Paseo del Prado. The Paseo was designed by King-Mayor Carlos III as a leafy nature walk with glorious fountains and a botanical garden for respite in scorching summers. As you walk east down Carrera de San Jerónimo toward the Paseo del Prado, consider that this was the route followed by Ferdinand and Isabella, the Catholic monarchs, over 500 years ago toward the church of **San Jerónimo el Real** (Moreto 4, behind Prado museum, tel. 91/420–3078). Used by the royal couple as a *retiro*, or place of meditation—hence the name of the nearby park—the church and cloisters were devastated in the Napoleonic Wars. Rebuilt in the late 19th century, the church is now open daily 8–1:30 and 5:30–8:30.

A Good Walk

Exit the **Puerta del Sol** ① into Calle de Alcalá, and you'll find on your left the **Real Academia de Bellas Artes de San Fernando** ⑯. Take the next right, past the elegant bank buildings, into Calle Sevilla and turn left at Plaza Canalejas (where La Violeta, at No. 6, sells violet-flavored sweets) into Carrera de San Jerónimo. (If you cross the plaza into Calle Príncipe, you'll reach the Plaza Santa Ana tapas-bar area.) Walk down San Jerónimo to Plaza de las Cortes. The granite building on the left with the lions is the Congreso, lower house of the Cortes, Spain's parliament.

Carrera de San Jerónimo leads you to the **Fuente de Neptuno** ⑰ in the wide Paseo del Prado. The renowned **Museo del Prado** ⑱ is across the plaza on the right. Immediately on your left is the **Museo Thyssen-Bornemisza** ⑲, and across the plaza on the left is the elegant Ritz Hotel, alongside the obelisk to all those who have died for Spain and, farther on, the Naval Museum. Here you have a choice: tackle one or both of these major museums now, or continue strolling.

Turning right and walking south on Paseo del Prado, you'll see the **Jardín Botánico** ⑳ on the left and eventually the **Atocha** train station, worth a quick visit for its humid indoor park, complete with tropical trees, benches, paths, and a pleasant restaurant. Across the traffic circle, the immense pile of painted tiles and winged statues houses the Ministerio de Agricultura (Agriculture Ministry). The **Centro de Arte Reina Sofía** ㉑, home to Picasso's *Guernica*, is in the building with the exterior glass elevators, best accessed by walking up Calle Atocha from the station and taking the first left.

Retracing your steps to the Fuente de Neptuno, turn right between the Ritz and the Prado. Straight ahead you'll see the **Casón del Buen Retiro** ㉒, on its left the **Museo del Ejército** ㉓, and farther on the vast **Parque del Retiro** ㉔.

Turning left at the Fuente de Neptuno will take you past the **Museo Thyssen-Bornemisza** ⑲ to the **Plaza de la Cibeles** ㉕, surrounded by the **Palacio de Comunicaciones** ㉖, now the post office; the **Banco de España** ㉗; and the **Casa de América** ㉘. Turn right at Cibeles, walk up Calle Alcalá, and you'll see Madrid's unofficial symbol, the **Puerta de Alcalá** ㉙, and, again, the Parque del Retiro. About 100 yards north of Cibeles, on the Paseo de Recoletos, the grand yellow mansion on the right, now a bank headquarters, was once the home of the Marquis of Salamanca, who at the turn of the 20th century built the exclusive shopping and residential neighborhood (northeast of here) that now bears his name. Continue north for the **Museo Arqueológico** ㉚, invaluable if you'll be traveling further in Spain, and the **Plaza Colón** ㉛.

TIMING

Including a visit to the Reina Sofía and a turn in the Parque del Retiro, you can make this walk in two to three hours. Set aside a morning or an afternoon *each* for return visits to the Prado and Thyssen-Bornemisza.

Sights to See

㉗ **BANCO DE ESPAÑA.** This massive 1884 building, Spain's central bank, takes up an entire block. It is said that the nation's gold reserves are held in great vaults that stretch under the Plaza de Cibeles traffic circle all the way to the fountain. The bank is not open to visitors, but if you can dodge traffic well enough to reach the median strip in front of it, you can take a fine photo of the fountain and the palaces with the Puerta de Alcalá arch in the background.

㉘ **CASA DE AMÉRICA.** A cultural center and art gallery focusing on Latin America, the Casa is housed in the allegedly haunted Palacio de Linares, built by a man who made his fortune in the New World and returned to a life of incestuous love and strange deaths. *Paseo Recoletos 2, tel. 91/595–4800. Palace tour 450 ptas.,* *gallery free. Gallery Tues.–Fri. 11–8, Sat. 11–7, Sun. 11–2; palace tours available Tues.–Fri. 9:30–11:30, weekends 10–1:30.*

㉒ CASÓN DEL BUEN RETIRO. This Prado annex is just a five-minute walk from the museum and is free with a Prado ticket. The building, once a ballroom, and the formal gardens in the Retiro are all that remain of Madrid's second royal complex, which filled the entire neighborhood until the early 19th century. On display are 19th-century Spanish paintings and sculpture, including works by Sorolla and Rusiñol. At press time the complex was scheduled to reopen in late 2001 after a regal restoration, with brand-new halls devoted to 17th- and 19th-century Spanish art. *C. Alfonso XII s/n, tel. 91/330–2867. Tues.–Sat. 9–7, Sun. 9–2.*

★ **㉑ CENTRO DE ARTE REINA SOFÍA** (Queen Sofia Art Center). Madrid's museum of modern art is housed in a converted hospital whose classical granite austerity is somewhat relieved (or ruined, depending on your point of view) by the two glass elevator shafts on the facade.

The collection focuses on Spain's three great modern masters: Pablo Picasso, Salvador Dalí, and Joan Miró. Take the elevator to the second floor to see the permanent collections; the other floors house visiting exhibits.

The first rooms are dedicated to the beginnings of Spain's modern movement and contain paintings from around the turn of the 20th century. The focal point is Picasso's 1901 *Woman in Blue*—hardly beautiful, but strikingly representational compared to his later works.

Moving on to the **Cubist** collection, which includes nine works by Juan Gris, be sure to see Dalí's splintered, blue-gray *Self-Portrait*, in which the artist depicts a few of his favorite things: a morning newspaper and a pack of cigarettes. The other highlight here is Picasso's *Musical Instruments on a Table*, one of many variations on this theme.

The Reina Sofía's showpiece is Picasso's famous **Guernica**, which occupies the center hall and is surrounded by dozens of studies for individual figures within it. The huge painting depicts the horror of the Nazi Condor Legion's bombing of the ancient Basque town of Guernica in 1937, a Civil War act that brought Spanish dictator Francisco Franco to power. The work—in many ways a 20th-century version of Goya's *The 3rd of May*—is something of a national shrine, as evidenced by the solemnity of Spaniards viewing it. The painting was not brought into Spain until 1981; Picasso, an ardent antifascist, refused to allow it to enter the country until democracy was restored.

The room in front of *Guernica* contains a collection of **surrealist** works, including six canvases by Miró, known for his childlike graphics. Opposite *Guernica* is a hall dedicated to Salvador Dalí, with paintings bequeathed to the government in the artist's will. Although Dalí is perhaps best known for works of a somewhat whimsical nature, many of these canvases are dark, haunting, and bursting with symbolism. Among the best known are *The Great Masturbator* (1929) and *The Enigma of Hitler* (1939), with its broken, dripping telephone.

The rest of the museum is devoted to more recent art, including the massive, gravity-defying sculpture *Toki Egin*, by Eduardo Chillida, considered Spain's greatest living sculptor, and five textural paintings by Barcelona artist Antoni Tàpies, whose works incorporate such materials as wrinkled sheets and straw. *Santa Isabel 52, tel. 91/467–5062. 400 ptas.; free Sat. after 2:30 and all day Sun. Mon. and Wed.–Sat. 10–9, Sun. 10–2:30.*

㉕ **FUENTE DE LA CIBELES** (Fountain of Cybele). A tree-lined walkway runs down the center of Paseo del Prado to the Plaza de la Cibeles, where this famous fountain depicts the nature goddess Cybele driving a chariot drawn by lions. Even more than the officially designated bear and strawberry tree, this monument, beautifully lighted at night, has come to symbolize Madrid—so much so that during the Civil War, patriotic Madrileños risked life and limb to sandbag it as Nationalist aircraft bombed the city.

⑰ FUENTE DE NEPTUNO (Neptune's Fountain). Just outside the Palace Hotel and the boutiques-filled Galerias del Prado, on the Plaza Canovas del Castillo, this fountain is at the hub of Madrid's Paseo del Arte, made up chiefly of the redbrick Prado Museum, stretched along the east side of the boulevard; the Thyssen-Bornemisza Museum, across the plaza; and, five blocks to the south, the Reina Sofía art center.

⑳ JARDÍN BOTÁNICO (Botanical Garden). Just south of the Prado Museum, the gardens provide a pleasant place to stroll or sit under the trees. True to the wishes of King Carlos III, they hold an array of plants, flowers, and cacti from around the world. *Plaza de Murillo 2, tel. 91/420–3017. 250 ptas. Summer, daily 10–9; winter, daily 10–6.*

㉚ MUSEO ARQUEOLÓGICO (Museum of Archaeology). The museum shares its neoclassical building with the **Biblioteca Nacional** (National Library). The biggest attraction here is a replica of the prehistoric cave paintings in Altamira, Cantabria, located underground in the garden. (Access to the real thing is highly restricted.) Inside the museum, look for the *Dama de Elche*, a bust of a wealthy, 4th-century Iberian woman, and notice that her headgear is a rough precursor to the mantillas and hair combs still associated with traditional Spanish dress. The ancient Visigothic votive crowns are another highlight, discovered in 1859 near Toledo and believed to date back to the 8th century. *C. Serrano 13, tel. 91/577–7912. 500 ptas.; free Sat. after 2:30 and all day Sun. Museum Tues.–Sat. 9:30–8:30, Sun. 9:30–2:30; reproduction cave paintings, Tues.–Sat. 11–2:30 and 5:30–6:30, Sun. 11–2:30.*

㉓ MUSEO DEL EJÉRCITO (Army Museum). A real treat for arms-and-armor buffs, this place is right on the museum mile. Among the 27,000 items on view are a sword that allegedly belonged to the Spanish hero El Cid; suits of armor; bizarre-looking pistols with

barrels capable of holding scores of bullets; Moorish tents; and
a cross carried by Christopher Columbus. It's an unusually
entertaining collection. *Mendez Nuñez 1, tel. 91/522–8977. 100
ptas. Tues.–Sun. 10–2.*

★ ⑱ **MUSEO DEL PRADO** (Prado Museum). When the Prado was
commissioned by King-Mayor Carlos III, in 1785, it was meant to
be a natural-science museum. The king, popularly remembered
as "Madrid's best mayor," wanted the museum, the adjoining
botanical gardens, and the elegant Paseo del Prado to serve as
a center of scientific enlightenment for his subjects. By the time
the building was completed in 1819, its purpose had changed to
exhibiting the vast collection of art gathered by Spanish royalty
since the time of Ferdinand and Isabella. The museum is now
adding a massive new wing, designed by Rafael Moneo, that will
resurrect long-hidden works by Zurbarán and Pereda and more
than double the number of paintings on display from the
permanent collection.

Painting is one of Spain's greatest contributions to world
culture, and the Prado's jewels are its works by the nation's
three great masters: Francisco Goya, Diego Velázquez, and El
Greco. The museum also holds masterpieces by Flemish and
Italian artists, collected when their lands were part of the
Spanish Empire. The museum benefited greatly from the
anticlerical laws of 1836, which forced monasteries, convents,
and churches to forfeit many of their artworks for public display.

Enter the Prado via the Goya entrance, with steps opposite the
Ritz Hotel, or the less-crowded Murillo door opposite the Jardín
Botánico. The layout varies (grab a floor plan), but the first halls
on the left, coming from the Goya entrance (7A to 11 on the
second floor, or *primera planta*) are usually devoted to **17th-
century Flemish painters** including Peter Paul Rubens (1577–
1640), Jacob Jordaens (1593–1678), and Antony van Dyck
(1599–1641).

Room 12 introduces you to the meticulous brushwork of **Velázquez** (1599–1660) in his numerous portraits of kings and queens. Look for the magnificent *Las Hilanderas* (*The Spinners*), evidence of the artist's talent for painting light. The Prado's most famous canvas, Velázquez's *Las Meninas* (*The Maids of Honor*), combines a self-portrait of the artist at work with a mirror reflection of the king and queen in a revolutionary interplay of space and perspectives. Picasso was obsessed with this work and painted several copies of it in his own abstract style, now on display in the Picasso Museum in Barcelona.

The south ends of the second and top floors (*planta primera* and *planta segunda*) are reserved for **Goya** (1746–1828), whose works span a staggering range of tone, from bucolic to horrific. Among his early masterpieces are portraits of the family of King Carlos IV, for whom he was court painter—one glance at their unflattering and imbecilic expressions, especially in the painting *The Family of Carlos IV*, reveals the loathing Goya developed for these self-indulgent, reactionary rulers. His famous side-by-side canvases, *The Clothed Maja* and *The Nude Maja*, may represent the young duchess of Alba, whom Goya adored and frequently painted. No one knows whether she ever returned his affection. The adjacent rooms house a series of idyllic scenes of Spaniards at play, painted as designs for tapestries.

Goya's paintings took on political purpose starting in 1808, when the population of Madrid rose up against occupying French troops. *The 2nd of May* portrays the insurrection at the Puerta del Sol, and its even more terrifying companion piece, *The 3rd of May*, depicts the nighttime executions of patriots who had rebelled the day before. The garish light effects in this work typify the romantic style, which favors drama over detail, and make it one of the most powerful indictments of violence ever committed to canvas.

Goya's "black paintings" are dark, disturbing works, completed late in his life, that reflect his inner turmoil after losing his hearing and his deep embitterment over the bloody War of Independence. These are copies of the monstrous hallucinatory paintings Goya made with marvelously free brush strokes on the walls of his house by the Río Manzanares, south of Madrid. Having grown terribly ill in his old age, Goya was deaf, lonely, bitter, and despairing; his terrifying *Saturn Devouring One of his Sons* probably represents the cruel, destructive forces of age and time.

Near the Goya entrance, the Prado's ground floor (*planta baja*) is filled with 15th- and 16th-century Flemish paintings, including the bizarre masterpiece *Garden of Earthly Delights*, by Hieronymous Bosch, recently restored. Next come Rooms 60A, 61A, and 62A, filled with the passionately spiritual works of **El Greco** (Doménikos Theotokópoulos, 1541–1614), the Greek-born artist who lived and worked in Toledo. El Greco is known for his mystical, elongated faces. His style was quite shocking to a public accustomed to strictly representational images; because he wanted his art to provoke emotion, El Greco is sometimes called the world's first "modern" painter. Two of his greatest paintings, *The Resurrection* and *The Adoration of the Shepherds*, are on view here. Before you leave, stop in the 14th- to 16th-century Italian rooms to see Titian's *Portrait of Emperor Charles V* and Raphael's exquisite *Portrait of a Cardinal*. Paseo del Prado s/n, tel. 91/420–3768. 500 ptas.; free Sat. after 2:30 and all day Sun. Tues.–Sat. 9–7, Sun. 9–2. www.museoprado.mcu.es

NEED A BREAK? **La Dolores** (Plaza de Jesús 4) is one of Madrid's most atmospheric old tiled bars, the perfect place for a beer or glass of wine and a plate of olives. It's a great alternative to the Prado's basement cafeteria and is just across the Paseo, then one block up on Calle Lope de Vega.

⓱ **MUSEO THYSSEN-BORNEMISZA.** Madrid's third and newest art center, with lots of space and natural light, occupies the

Villahermosa Palace, finished in 1771. This ambitious collection of 800 paintings traces the history of Western art through examples from every important movement, beginning with 13th-century Italy.

The works were gathered from the 1920s on by industrialist Baron Hans Heinrich Thyssen-Bornemisza and his father. At the urging of his Spanish wife (a former Miss Spain), the baron agreed to donate the collection to Spain. Critics have described the collection as the minor works of major artists and the major works of minor artists, but the museum itself is beautiful, and its Impressionist paintings are the only ones on display in the country.

One of the high points here is Hans Holbein's *Portrait of Henry VIII* (purchased from the late Princess Diana's grandfather, who used the money to buy a new Bugatti sports car). American artists are also well represented; look for the Gilbert Stuart portrait of George Washington's cook, and note how closely the composition and rendering resembles the artist's famous painting of the Founding Father himself. Two halls are devoted to the Impressionists and post-Impressionists, including many works by Pissarro and a few each by Renoir, Monet, Degas, Van Gogh, and Cézanne.

Within 20th-century art, the baron shows a proclivity for terror-filled (albeit dynamic and colorful) German expressionism, but there are also some soothing works by Georgia O'Keeffe and Andrew Wyeth. *Paseo del Prado 8, tel. 91/369–0151. 700 ptas. Tues.– Sun. 10–7.*

㉖ PALACIO DE COMUNICACIONES. This ornate building on the southeast side of Plaza de Cibeles is Madrid's main post office. *Stamps weekdays 9 AM–10 PM, Sat. 9–8, Sun. 10–1; phone, telex, telegrams, and fax weekdays 8 AM–midnight, weekends 8 AM–10 PM.*

★ ☙ ㉔ **PARQUE DEL RETIRO** (literally, the Retreat). Once the private playground of royalty, Madrid's crowning park is a vast expanse of green encompassing formal gardens, fountains, lakes, exhibition halls, children's play areas, outdoor cafés, and a **Puppet Theater,** featuring free slapstick routines that even non–Spanish speakers will enjoy. Shows take place on Saturday at 1 and on Sunday at 1, 6, and 7. The park is especially lively on weekends, when it fills with street musicians, jugglers, clowns, gypsy fortune-tellers, and sidewalk painters along with hundreds of Spanish families out for a walk. The park hosts a monthlong book fair in May and occasional flamenco concerts in summer.

From the entrance at the Puerta de Alcalá, head straight toward the center and you'll find the **Estanque** (lake), presided over by a grandiose equestrian statue of King Alfonso XII, erected by his mother. Just behind the lake, north of the statue, is one of the best of the park's many cafés. If you're feeling energetic, you can rent a boat and work up an appetite just rowing around the lake.

The 19th-century **Palacio de Cristal** (Crystal Palace), southeast of the Estanque, was built to house a collection of exotic plants from the Philippines, a Spanish possession at the time. This airy marvel of steel and glass sits on a base of decorative tile. Next door is a small lake with ducks and swans. At the south end of the park, along the Paseo del Uruguay, is the **Rosaleda** (rose garden), an English garden bursting with color and heavy with floral scents for most of the summer. West of the Rosaleda, look for a statue called the **Ángel Caído** (Fallen Angel), which Madrileños claim is the only one in the world depicting the prince of darkness before (during, actually) his fall from grace.

③ **PLAZA COLÓN.** This modern plaza is named for Christopher Columbus. A statue of the explorer (identical to one in Barcelona's port) looks west from a high tower in the middle of the square. Beneath the massive plaza is the **Centro Cultural de la Villa** (tel. 91/575–6080), a new performing-arts facility. Behind Plaza Colón is **Calle Serrano,** the city's premier shopping street (think Gucci, Prada, and Loewe). Take a stroll in either direction on Serrano for some window-shopping.

NEED A
BREAK? **El Espejo** comprises two classy bars near the Plaza Colón—one in an original Belle Epoque setting on a side street, the other in a splendid pavilion of glass and wrought iron in the middle of the Paseo de Recoletos. Pull up a chair on the shady terrace or sit in the air-conditioned, stained-glass bar to rest your feet and sip a cup of coffee or a beer. *Paseo de Recoletos 31, tel. 91/308–2347. Daily* 10 AM–2 AM.

㉙ **PUERTA DE ALCALÁ.** This triumphal arch was built by Carlos III in 1778 to mark the site of one of the ancient city gates. You can still see the bomb damage inflicted on the arch during the civil war.

⑯ **REAL ACADEMIA DE BELLAS ARTES DE SAN FERNANDO** (St. Ferdinand Academy of Fine Arts). Designed by Churriguera in the waning Baroque years of the early 18th century, this little-visited museum is a showcase of painting and, to a lesser extent, the decorative arts. The same building houses the **Instituto de Calcografía** (Prints Institute), which sells limited-edition prints from original plates engraved by Spanish artists, including Goya. *Alcalá 13, tel. 91/522–0046. 400 ptas.; free weekends. Tues.–Fri. 9:30–7, Sat.–Mon. 9:30–2.*

OLD MADRID

Plaza Mayor ⑮. Looking up at the erotic mural, exit under the large arch to the far left and walk down Ciudad Rodrigo, then turn left. Across the road is a restored market; down **Cava de San Miguel** ㉜ you'll see tapas bars that go deep into caves under the Plaza Mayor. The entrance to **Las Cuevas de Luis Candelas** (☞ Eating Out) is on the left, by the steps up to the Plaza Mayor. Farther down, at Cuchilleros 17, is the historic restaurant Botín. Cross the Plaza de Puerta Cerrada and you'll see an alleyway, Nuncio, on the right: down here on the left is the **Palacio de la Nunciatura.**

Nuncio widens, and on your left at No. 17 is the Taberna de Cien Vinos, a good place to sample Spanish wine. Opposite the tavern is the church of San Pedro el Viejo (St. Peter the Elder), one of Madrid's oldest, with a Mudéjar tower. Bear right and enter Príncipe Anglona to enter **Plaza de la Paja** ㉝. Down on the right is the **Costanilla de San Andrés,** which leads to Calle Segovia and a view of the viaduct above. At the top of Plaza de la Paja is the church of San Andrés; turn right after the church down Carrera San Francisco to visit the **Basílica de San Francisco el Grande** ㉞. Backtrack and turn left after San Andrés down **Cava Baja**—this curving street is packed with bars and restaurants. Casa Lucio, at No. 35, is a favorite of the king; opposite is La Solea, with late-night jazz and, upstairs, flamenco singing. La Chata at No. 24, is a fun Madrid *tasca* (tavern). Continue straight ahead to return to Plaza Mayor.

TIMING

This 90-minute walk requires some short uphill climbs through the winding streets. Allow ample time for stops to absorb the Old World charm—especially in summer, when heat will be a factor.

Sights to See

㉞ **BASÍLICA DE SAN FRANCISCO EL GRANDE.** In 1760, Carlos III built this impressive basilica on the site of a Franciscan convent, allegedly founded by St. Francis of Assisi in 1217. The dome, 108 ft in diameter, is the largest in Spain, even larger than that of St. Paul's in London, where its 19 bells were cast in 1882. The seven main doors were carved of American walnut by Casa Juan Guas. Three chapels adjoin the circular church, the most famous being that of **San Bernardino de Siena**, which contains a Goya masterpiece depicting a preaching San Bernardino. The figure standing on the right, not looking up, is a self-portrait of Goya. The 16th-century Gothic choir stalls came from La Cartuja del Paular, in rural Segovia province. *Pl. de San Francisco, tel. 91/365–3400. Free. Tues.–Fri. 11–12:30 and 4–6:30.*

★ ③② **CAVA DE SAN MIGUEL.** The narrow, picturesque streets behind the Plaza de la Villa are well worth exploring. From the Plaza Mayor, turn onto the Plaza de San Miguel, with the glass-and-iron San Miguel market on your right. Proceed down Cava de San Miguel past the row of **ancient tapas bars** built right into the retaining wall of the plaza above. Each one specializes in a different food: *Mesón de champiñones* (mushrooms), *Mesón de boquerónes* (anchovies), *Mesón de tortilla* (excellent Spanish omelets), and so on. Madrileños and travelers alike flock here each evening to sample the food and sing along with raucous musicians, who delight in playing non-Spanish tunes for the presumed delight of tourists.

COSTANILLA DE SAN ANDRÉS. This ramped street leads up from Calle Segovia to the heart of the old city, the Plaza de la Paja. Look down the narrow Calle Príncipe Anglona for a good view of the Mudéjar tower on the church of **San Pedro el Viejo** (St. Peter the Elder), one of the city's oldest. The brick tower is believed to have been built in 1354 following the Christian reconquest of Algeciras, near Gibraltar. Notice the tiny defensive slits, designed to accommodate crossbows.

LAS CUEVAS DE LUIS CANDELAS. The oldest of Madrid's taverns, about halfway down Cava de San Miguel, is named for a 19th-century Madrid version of Robin Hood, famous for his ingenious ways of tricking the rich out of their money and jewels. As Cava de San Miguel becomes Calle Cuchilleros, you'll see **Botín** on the left, Madrid's oldest restaurant and a onetime haunt of Ernest Hemingway (☞ Eating Out). The curving Cuchilleros was once a moat just outside the city walls. The plaza with the bright murals at the intersection of Calle Segovia is called the **Puerta Cerrada** (Cava San Miguel and Calle Cuchilleros), or Closed Gate, named for the city gate that once stood here.

PALACIO DE LA NUNCIATURA (Palace of the Nunciat). Near the Plaza Puerta Cerrada off Calle Segovia, one of Madrid's main medieval streets, this mansion once housed the Pope's ambassadors to Spain. It's not open to the public, but you can peek inside the Renaissance garden. *Costanilla del Nuncio s/n.*

NEED A BREAK? The **Café del Nuncio** (Costanilla del Nuncio s/n), on the corner of Calle Segovia, is a relaxing Old World place for a coffee or beer against a backdrop of classical music.

33 PLAZA DE LA PAJA. Located at the top of the hill, on Costanilla San Andrés, the Plaza de la Paja was the most important square in medieval Madrid. Although a few upscale restaurants have moved in, this little square retains its own atmosphere. The plaza's jewel is the **Capilla del Obispo** (Bishop's Chapel), built between 1520 and 1530; this was where peasants deposited their tithes, called *diezmas*—literally, one-tenth of their crop. The stacks of wheat on the chapel's ceramic tiles refer to this tradition. Architecturally, the chapel marks a transition from the blockish Gothic period, which gave the structure its basic shape, to the Renaissance, the source of the decorations. Try to get inside to see the intricately carved polychrome altarpiece by Francisco Giralta, featuring scenes from the life of Christ. Opening hours are erratic; the best time to visit is during mass or on feast days.

The chapel forms part of the complex of the domed church of **San Andrés,** built to house the remains of Madrid's male patron saint, San Isidro Labrador. Isidro was a peasant who worked fields belonging to the Vargas family. The 16th-century **Vargas palace** forms the eastern side of the Plaza de la Paja. According to legend, St. Isidro actually worked little but had the best-tended fields thanks to many hours of prayer. When Señor Vargas came out to investigate the phenomenon, Isidro made a spring of sweet water spurt from the ground to quench his master's thirst. Because St. Isidro's power had to do with water, his remains were paraded through the city in times of drought in the hope that he would bring rain, as recently as the turn of the 20th century.

CASTIZO MADRID

The Spanish word *castizo* means "authentic," and *los Madrileños castizos* are the Spanish equivalent of London's cockneys. There are few "sights" in the usual sense on this route; instead, you wander through some of Madrid's most traditional and lively neighborhoods. Within these are a growing number of recent immigrants and the attendant employment problems. Muggings are not uncommon, so think twice about this walk if you don't feel reasonably streetwise.

A Good Walk

Begin at the **Plaza Santa Ana** ㉟, the hub of the theater district in the 17th century and now a center of nocturnal activity, not all of it desirable. The dusty plaza is rimmed by a number of notable buildings, including the **Teatro Español** and the tiled **Casa de Guadalajara.** Walk east two blocks on Calle del Prado and turn right on Calle León, named for a lion kept here long ago by a resident Moor. One block on this street brings you to the corner of **Calle Cervantes,** where the author of *Don Quixote* and the "Spanish Shakespeare" lived in what are now called the **Casa de Cervantes** ㊱ and the **Casa de Lope de Vega.**

One block farther on Calle León, turn left on Calle de las Huertas, the premier bar strip in bar-speckled Madrid. One block down Huertas, turn right onto Calle Amor de Dios and walk to its end, at the busy Calle Atocha. Across the street you'll see the church of **San Nicolás.** To the left of the church, walk down **Pasaje Doré** through the Anton Martín morning market, a colorful assortment of market stalls typical of most Madrid neighborhoods.

Turn right on Calle Santa Isabel, by the **Cine Doré** ㊲, and take your first left on Calle de la Rosa—which, after a jog to the right, becomes Calle de la Cabeza. You'll pass the restaurant Casa Lastra (☞ Eating Out). On the southwest corner with Calle Lavapiés is the site of the **Cárcel de la Inquisición** ㊳. Turn left here: this is the beginning of the **Barrio Lavapiés,** Madrid's old *Judería* (Jewish Quarter). Lavapiés remains one of Madrid's most castizo working-class neighborhoods, though gentrification is beginning to creep in; the streets have been recobbled, and lighting improved. Explore side streets off Calle Lavapiés, then continue down and south until you reach the heart of the neighborhood, **Plaza Lavapiés** ㊴.

Leave the plaza heading west on Calle Sombrerete. After two blocks you'll reach the intersection of Calle Mesón de Paredes, on which corner you'll see a lovingly preserved example of a popular Madrid architecture, the **Corrala building** ㊵. Life in this type of balconied apartment building is very public, with laundry flapping in the breeze, babies crying, and old women gossiping over the railings. Neighbors once shared common kitchen and bath facilities in the patio.

Work your way west, crossing Calle de Embajadores into the neighborhood known as **El Rastro** ㊶—a shopper's paradise, with streets of small family stores selling furniture, antiques, and a cornucopia of used junk (some of it greatly overpriced). On Sunday, El Rastro becomes a flea market, and Calle de Ribera de Curtidores, the steep main drag, is closed to traffic, jammed with outdoor booths, shoppers, and pickpockets.

TIMING
Allow at least three hours. The point of this walk is really the atmosphere. Any weekday morning is a good time to browse the Anton Martín market; the streets surrounding the Plaza Santa Ana are more interesting after dark, as they're lined with some of Madrid's best tapas bars and nightspots. El Rastro can be saved for a Sunday morning if you decide to brave the crowds at the flea market.

Sights to See

BARRIO LAVAPIÉS. The Barrio Lavapiés is the old *Judería*. Like Moors, Jews were forced to live outside the city walls after the

Christian reconquest hit Madrid in 1085, and this was one of the suburbs they founded.

38 **CÁRCEL DE LA INQUISICIÓN** (Inquisition Jail). Unmarked by any historical plaque, the former jail at the southeast corner of Calle Cabeza and Calle Lavapiés is now a large tapas bar, the **Taberna del Avapiés,** named for the old Jewish quarter. Here Jews, Moors, and others designated unrepentant heathens or sinners bent to the inquisitors' whims; the prison later became a Cárcel de la Corona (Crown Prison) for the incarceration of wayward soldiers, priests, and nuns. Ask a bartender if you can see the original, two-story medieval patio out back—it's tiny, but highly evocative.

36 **CASA DE CERVANTES.** A plaque marks the house where the author of *Don Quixote* lived and died. Miguel de Cervantes' 1605 epic story of the man with the impossible dream is one of the most widely translated and read books in the world. *C. Cervantes and C. León.*

CASA DE LOPE DE VEGA. The home of Lope de Vega, a contemporary of Cervantes', has been turned into a museum that shows how a house of that period was typically furnished. Considered the Shakespeare of Spanish literature, Lope de Vega (1562–1635) wrote some 1,800 plays and enjoyed great success during his lifetime. *C. Cervantes 11, tel. 91/429–9216. 200 ptas. Sept.–July, weekdays 9:30–2, Sat. 10–2.*

NEED A **Taberna de Antonio Sánchez.** Drop into Madrid's oldest bar for
BREAK? a glass of wine and some tapas, or just a peek. The dark walls (lined with bullfighting paintings), zinc bar, and pulley system used to lift casks of wine from the cellar look much the same as they did when the place first opened in 1830. Meals are also served in a dining room in the back. Specialties include *rabo de buey* (bull's-tail stew) and *morcillo al horno* (a beef stew). *Mesón de Paredes 13.*

37 CINE DORÉ. A rare example of Art Nouveau architecture in Madrid, the hip Cine Doré shows movies from the Spanish National Film Archives and eclectic foreign films, usually in the original language. Show times are listed in newspapers under FILMOTECA. The lobby, trimmed with smart pink neon, has a sleek café-bar and a good bookshop. *C. Santa Isabel 3, tel. 91/369–1125. Tues.–Sun.; hrs vary depending on show times.*

40 CORRALA BUILDING. This structure is not unlike the *corrales* that were used as Madrid's early theaters; there's even a plaque here to remind you that the setting for the famous 19th-century *zarzuela* (light opera) *La Revoltosa* was a *corrala* like this one. City-sponsored musical-theater events are occasionally held here in summer. The ruins across the street were once the **Escalopíos de San Fernando,** one of several churches and parochial schools that fell victim to anti-Catholic sentiments in this neighborhood during the Civil War. *C. Mesón de Paredes and C. Sombrerete.*

41 EL RASTRO. Filled with tiny shops selling antiques and all manner of used stuff, some of it junk, the Rastro becomes an overcrowded flea market on Sunday morning from 10 to 2. The best time to explore is any other morning, when a little browsing and bargaining are likely to turn up such treasures as old iron grillwork, marble tabletops, or gilt picture frames. The main street of the Rastro is Ribera de Curtidores; the best streets for browsing are the ones to the west.

39 PLAZA LAVAPIÉS. The heart of the historic Jewish *barrio*, this picturesque plaza remains a neighborhood hub. To the left is the Calle de la Fe (Street of Faith), which was called Calle Sinagoga until the expulsion of the Jews in 1492. The church of **San Lorenzo** at the end was built on the site of the razed synagogue. Legend has it that Jews and Moors who chose baptism over exile were forced to walk up this street barefoot to the ceremony to demonstrate the sincerity of their new faith. *Top of C. de la Fe.*

③⑤ PLAZA SANTA ANA. This plaza was the heart of the theater district in the 17th century—the golden age of Spanish literature—and is now the center of Madrid's thumping nightlife. A statue of 15th-century playwright Pedro Calderón de la Barca delivering one of his own lines faces the **Teatro Español.** Inscribed with the names of Spain's greatest playwrights and rebuilt in 1980 following a fire, the theater stands in the same place where plays were performed as early as the 16th century, at that time in a rowdy outdoor setting called a *corrala*. These makeshift theaters were usually installed in a vacant lot between two apartment buildings, and families with balconies overlooking the action rented out seats to wealthy patrons of the arts. Opposite the theater, the **Villa Rosa,** with a facade of ceramic tile, is currently a popular nightspot. The **Hotel Reina Victoria** was not always so upscale but has always been favored by bullfighters, including Manolete. Off to the side of the hotel is the diminutive **Plaza del Ángel,** home to one of Madrid's best jazz clubs, the Café Central. Back on the Plaza Santa Ana is one of Madrid's most famous cafés, the **Cervecería Alemana,** another Hemingway hangout. It still attracts struggling writers, poets, and beer drinkers.

SAN NICOLÁS. The predecessor of this plain, modern church was burned in 1936, a story vividly described by writer Arturo Barea in his autobiographical book *The Forge*. Little of the original structure remains. Like many other churches during that turbulent period, the original church of St. Nicholas fell to the wrath of working-class crowds who felt they were the victims of centuries of clerical oppression. *C. Atocha and Plaza Anton Martín.*

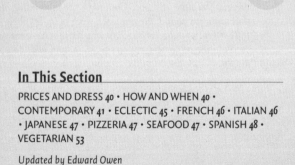

In This Section

Updated by Edward Owen

eating out

AS CAPITAL OF THE REALM and home of the king since the 16th century, Madrid has attracted generations of courtiers, diplomats, politicians, and tradesmen, all of whom have brought their own culinary tastes and styles from other parts of Spain and from abroad. Madrid's best restaurants specialize in Basque cooking, Spain's haute cuisine, while numerous seafood houses, as if compulsively craving the distant sea, take full advantage of the abundant fish and shellfish trucked in nightly from both the Atlantic and the Mediterranean coasts. Madrid has long been known as Spain's "first port," the immediate destination of most of the finest produce from Spain's fishing fleet—by far the largest in Europe.

Madrid's own cuisine is based on the roasts and thick soups and stews of Castile, Spain's high central *meseta* (plain). Roast suckling pig and lamb are standard Madrid feasts, as are baby goat and chunks of beef from Ávila. *Cocido madrileño* (garbanzo-bean stew) and *callos a la madrileña* (stewed tripe) are fundamental local specialties. Cocido is a delicious and hearty winter meal consisting of garbanzo beans, vegetables, potatoes, sausages, and pork. The best cocidos are slowly simmered in earthenware crocks over open fires and served as a complete meal in several courses: first the broth, which comes with angel-hair pasta; then the beans and vegetables; and finally the meat. You can order cocido in the most elegant restaurants as well as the humblest holes-in-the-wall, and it's usually offered as a midday selection on Monday or Wednesday.Callos are a much simpler concoction of veal tripe stewed with tomatoes, onions, hot paprika, and garlic.

Jamón serrano (cured ham)—a specialty from the livestock lands of Teruel, Extremadura, and Andalusia—has become a staple in Madrid; wanderers are likely to come across a *museo del jamón* (literally, ham museum), where endless legs of the dried delicacy dangle in store windows or in bars. Restaurant windows betray a local affinity for pork products in general, particularly hams and baby suckling pigs. As for fast food, busy Madrileños grab a *bocadillo* (sandwich) from a stand for a quick bite.

Although the countryside near the capital produces some wines, these are less than exceptional. The house wine in most basic Madrid restaurants is a sturdy, uncomplicated Valdepeñas from La Mancha. A traditional, anise-flavored liqueur (*anís*) is produced outside the village of Chinchón.

PRICES AND DRESS

Dress in most Madrid restaurants and tapas bars is casual but stylish. The pricier places are on the formal side; men often wear jackets and ties, and women often wear skirts. (Note that throughout the chapter dress is mentioned only when men are required to wear a jacket or a jacket and tie.)

CATEGORY	COST*
$$$$	over 6,000 ptas.
$$$	4,000–6,000 ptas.
$$	1,800–4,000 ptas.
$	under 1,800 ptas.

per person for three-course meal, excluding drinks, service, and tax

HOW AND WHEN

Most restaurants don't serve breakfast (*desayuno*); for coffee and carbohydrates, head to a bar or *cafetería*. Outside major hotels, which serve buffet breakfasts, breakfast in Spain is usually limited to coffee and toast or a roll. Lunch (*comida* or *almuerzo*) traditionally consists of an appetizer, a main course, and dessert, followed by coffee and perhaps a liqueur. Between lunch and dinner the best way to snack is to sample some *tapas* (appetizers) at a bar; normally you can choose from quite a variety. Dinner (*cena*) is somewhat lighter, with perhaps only one course.

In addition to an à la carte menu, most restaurants offer a daily fixed-price menu (*menú del día*) consisting of two courses, coffee, and dessert at a very attractive price. If the server does not suggest the menú del día when you're seated (perhaps on the assumption that foreigners will order à la carte), feel free to ask for it—"Hay menú del día, por favor?"

Madrileños tend to eat their meals even later than other Spaniards, and that's saying something. Restaurants generally open for lunch at 1:30 and fill up by 3. Dinnertime begins at 9, but reservations for 11 are common, and a meal can be a wonderfully lengthy (up to three hours) affair. Restaurants perform equally well at lunchtime, when most places offer a menú del día (daily fixed-price special), which includes a main course, wine, dessert, wine, and coffee. If you're not a night owl, make the most of the early-evening tapas hour and try to defy your body clock for at least one night: a late dinner here is the only kind.

Credit cards are widely accepted in Spanish restaurants. If you pay bycredit card, leave the tip in cash.

CONTEMPORARY

$$$$ **VIRIDIANA.** The trendiest of Madrid's top restaurants, Viridiana has a relaxed, somewhat cramped bistro atmosphere and black-and-white decor punctuated by prints from Luis Buñuel's classic anticlerical film (for which the place is named). Iconoclast chef Abraham Garcia says "market-based" is too narrow a description for his creative menu, though the list does change every two

madrid dining

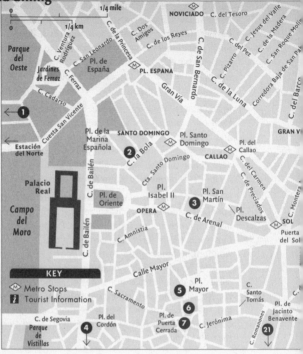

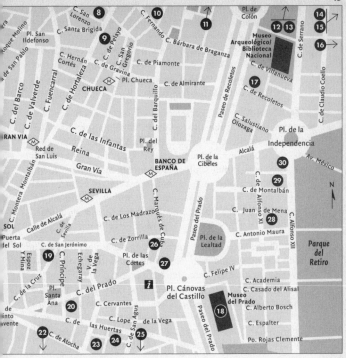

weeks depending on what's locally available. You might find red onions stuffed with *morcilla* (black pudding); soft flour tortillas wrapped around marinated fresh tuna; or filet mignon in white truffle sauce. If it's available, try the superb duck pâté drizzled with sherry and served with Tokay wine. The tangy grapefruit sherbet is a marvel. *Juan de Mena 14, tel. 91/531–5222. Reservations essential. AE, DC, MC, V. Closed Sun., Holy Week, and Aug.*

$$$$ ZALACAÍN. A deep-apricot color scheme, set off by dark wood and
★ gleaming silver, makes this restaurant look like an exclusive villa. Zalacaín introduced nouvelle cuisine to Spain and continues to set the pace 20 years later. Splurge on dishes like prawn salad in avocado vinaigrette, scallops and leeks in Albariño wine, and roast pheasant with truffles; or sample the chef's own choices with a tasting menu. Service is somewhat stuffy, and jackets are required. *Alvarez de Baena 4, tel. 91/561–5935. Reservations essential. AE, DC, V. Closed Sun., Aug., and Holy Week. No lunch Sat.*

$$$ IROCO. This large, stylish, green-walled establishment is popular with businesspeople at the lunch hour and trendy folk in the evening. In summer, reservations are essential for tables on the garden patio, where Crown Prince Felipe has been spotted. The *nueva cocina* (nouvelle cuisine) is well presented, and the set lunch menu is good value. Classic dishes include prawn rolls, hake in green asparagus sauce, and chocolate mousse. *Velázquez 18, tel. 91/431–7381. Reservations essential. AE, DC, MC, V.*

$$$ LA CAVA REAL. Wine connoisseurs love the intimate atmosphere of this small bar-restaurant, which was Madrid's first true wine bar when it opened in 1983. Still part of Spain's largest wine club (Warning: no beer!), it's also open to the public, smartly decorated in plush reds and dark browns. There are a staggering 350 wines on offer, including 50 by the glass. The charming and experienced maître d', Chema Gómez, can help you choose. Chef Javier Collar designs good-value menus around various wines, and the à la carte selection is plentiful, mainly *nueva cocina* with game in season as well as fancy desserts and cheeses. *Espronceda 34, tel. 91/442–5432. Reservations essential. AE, DC, MC, V. Closed Sun. and Aug.*

$$ CASA VALLEJO. With its homey dining room, friendly staff, creative menu, and reasonable prices, Casa Vallejo is a well-kept secret of Madrid's low-budget foodies. Try the tomato, zucchini, and cheese tart or artichokes and clams to start; follow up with duck breast in prune sauce or meatballs made with lamb, almonds, and pine nuts. The fudge-and-raspberry pie alone is worth the trip. *San Lorenzo 9, tel. 91/308–6158. Reservations essential. MC, V. Closed Sun. No dinner Mon.*

$$ LA GAMELLA. ★ American-born chef Dick Stephens has created a new, reasonably priced menu at this perennially popular dinner spot. The sophisticated rust-red dining room, batik tablecloths, oversize plates, and attentive service remain the same, but much of the nouvelle cuisine has been replaced by more traditional fare, such as chicken in garlic, beef bourguignon, and steak tartare à la Jack Daniels. A few of the old signature dishes, like sausage-and-red-pepper quiche and bittersweet chocolate pâté, remain. The lunchtime *menú del día* is a great value. *Alfonso XII 4, tel. 91/532–4509. AE, DC, MC, V. Closed Sun. and Aug. 15–30. No lunch Sat.*

ECLECTIC

$$$ EL CENADOR DEL PRADO. ★ The name means "The Prado Dining Room," and the settings are a Baroque salon and a plant-filled conservatory. The Cenador's innovative menu has French and Asian touches, as well as exotic Spanish dishes that rarely appear in restaurants. The house specialty is *patatas a la importancia* (sliced potatoes fried in a sauce of garlic, parsley, and clams); other possibilities include shellfish consommé with ginger ravioli, veal and eggplant in béchamel, and venison with prunes. For dessert try the *bartolillos*, custard-filled pastries. *C. del Prado 4, tel. 91/429–1561. AE, DC, MC, V. Closed Sun. and Aug. 1–15. No lunch Sat.*

$$ **CORNUCOPIA EN DESCALZAS.** Owned by two Americans, a Frenchman, and a Spaniard, this young, friendly restaurant on the second floor of an old mansion (just off the Plaza de las Descalzas Reales) serves what it calls Euro-American cuisine. The menu changes with the season; possibilities include grilled entrecote marinated in bourbon and honey, bream on a dill compote, and stewed rabbit with tomatoes, onion, and thyme. In winter, the restaurant becomes a tearoom Saturday and Sunday from 5 to 8. *Flora 1, tel. 91/547–6465. AE, MC, V. Closed Easter wk and last two wks in Aug.*

FRENCH

$$$ **EL BORBOLLÓN.** For nearly two decades the friendly Castro family has run this elegant yet comfortable restaurant and bar between Paseo de Recoletos and Calle Serrano, decorated with pink tablecloths, fresh flowers, and paintings of country scenes. Chef Eduardo prepares French-Basque cuisine, with specialties including various crepes, *carré* (a prime cutlet or chop) of lamb, fresh sea bass, turbot, and hake, plus rich game dishes in season. Alfonso Castro, the knowledgeable sommelier, offers good wines and brandies. Dinner reservations are wise; at lunchtime, there's food at the bar. *Recoletos 7, tel. 91/431–4134. AE, DC, MC, V. Closed Sun. and Aug.*

ITALIAN

$$$ **CIAO.** Always noisy and packed with happy diners, Ciao is Madrid's best Italian restaurant. Homemade pastas, like tagliatelle with wild mushrooms and *panzarotti* stuffed with spinach and ricotta, are popular as inexpensive main courses; but the kitchen also turns out credible versions of osso buco and veal scallopini, accompanied by a good selection of Italian wines. The decor—mirrored walls and sleek black furniture—convincingly evokes fashionable Milan. A second location (Apodaca 20, tel. 91/447–0036), run by the owner's sons and daughter, also serves pizza. *Argensola 7, tel. 91/308–2519. Reservations essential. AE, DC, MC, V. Closed Sun. No lunch Sat.*

JAPANESE

$$$ GINZA SUSHI BAR. Madrid's first Japanese sushi bar, Ginza opened at the end of 1999, handily located opposite American Express and the Palace Hotel, near the Thyssen and Prado museums. The conveyor belt does a brisk business, with plates priced between 200 and 850 ptas., and there's a sit-down restaurant upstairs. The staff is cheerful, and Spain's fresh fish is perfect for the tasty morsels. You can reserve seats at the bar. *Plaza de las Cortes 3, tel. 91/429–7619. AE, DC, MC, V. Closed Mon.*

PIZZERIA

$$ NABUCCO. With pastel-washed walls and subtle lighting from gigantic, wrought-iron candelabras, this pizzeria and trattoria is a trendy but elegant haven in gritty Chueca. Fresh bread sticks and garlic olive oil show up within minutes of your arrival. The spinach, ricotta, and walnut ravioli is heavenly, and this may be the only Italian restaurant in Madrid where you can order (California-style?) barbecued-chicken pizza, although the four-cheese one is good as well. Considering the ambience and quality, the bill is a pleasant surprise. *Hortaleza 108, tel. 91/310–0611. AE, MC, V.*

SEAFOOD

$$$ EL PESCADOR. Locals swear that seafood served in Madrid is
★ fresher than in the coastal towns where it was caught. That's probably an exaggeration, but El Pescador, one of Madrid's most respected seafood restaurants, makes it seem plausible. Stop for a drink at the bar and savor the aromas wafting from the kitchen, where skilled chefs dressed in fishermen's smocks prepare shellfish just behind the counter. Among the tapas, the *salpicón de mariscos* (mussels, lobster, shrimp, and onions in vinaigrette) is incredible. The best dish on the dinner menu is *lenguado Evaristo* (grilled sole), named for the restaurant's owner. When it's busy, the place can be cheerful and noisy, with dockside-

rustic decor: lobster-pot lamps, red-and-white-check tablecloths, and rough-hewn posts and beams. Unfortunately, the aging waiters can be disagreeably surly. *José Ortega y Gasset 75, tel. 91/402–1290. MC, V. Closed Sun. and Aug.*

$$$ LA TRAINERA. With its nautical decor and maze of little dining rooms, this informal restaurant is all about fresh seafood—the best money can buy. Crab, lobster, shrimp, mussels, and a dozen other types of shellfish are served by weight in *raciones* (large portions). Although many Spanish diners share several plates of these shellfish as their entire meal, the grilled hake, sole, or turbot makes an unbeatable second course. Skip the listless house wine and go for a bottle of Albariño from the cellar. *Lagasca 60, tel. 91/576–8035. AE, MC, V. Closed Sun. and Aug.*

SPANISH

$$$$ CASINO DE MADRID–LA TERRAZA. This rooftop terrace just off
★ Puerta del Sol offers two rare opportunities: to see the richly ornamented interior of one of Madrid's oldest and most exclusive clubs (the Casino was a club for gentlemen, not gamblers), and to sample the culinary inventions of Ferrán Adriá, one of the most inventive chefs in Europe. Adriá is not present—he runs his own famous restaurant, El Bulli, near Roses in Catalonia—but his exquisite dishes are. His trademarks are the lightest and tastiest of mousses, and ravioli in rare flavors that explode in the mouth. For the gamut of epicurean titillation, splurge on the 11-plate tasting menu, 10,000 ptas. per gastronome. On warm evenings the terrace is stunning. *Alcalá 15, tel. 91/532–1275. Reservations essential. AE, DC, MC, V. Closed Sun. and Aug. No lunch Sat.*

$$$$ HORCHER. Housed in a luxurious mansion at the edge of the
★ Parque del Retiro, this classic restaurant is renowned for hearty but elegant fare served with impeccable style. Specialties include the kinds of game dishes traditionally favored by Spanish aristocracy: wild boar, venison, roast wild duck with almond

croquettes. The star appetizer is lobster salad with truffles. Dishes like Stroganoff with mustard, pork chops with sauerkraut, and *baumkuchen* (a chocolate-covered fruit and cake dessert) reflect the restaurant's Germanic roots. (The Horcher family operated a restaurant in Berlin at the turn of the 20th century.) The intimate dining room is decorated with rust-colored brocade and antique Austrian porcelain, and a wide selection of French and German wines rounds out the menu. Jacket and tie are required. *Alfonso XII 6, tel. 91/522–0731. Reservations essential. AE, DC, MC, V. Closed Sun. and Aug. No lunch Sat.*

$$$$ LHARDY. Serving Madrid specialties in the same central location for more than 150 years, Lhardy looks pretty much the same as it must have on day one, with its dark-wood paneling, brass chandeliers, and red-velvet chairs. The menu offers international fare, but most diners come for the traditional cocido a la madrileña and callos a la madrileña. Game, sea bass in champagne sauce, and dessert soufflés are also finely prepared. The dining rooms are upstairs; the ground-floor entry doubles as a delicatessen and stand-up coffee bar that fills on chilly winter mornings with shivering souls sipping steaming-hot *caldo* (chicken broth) from silver urns. *Carrera de San Jerónimo 8, tel. 91/522–2207. AE, DC, MC, V. No dinner Sun.*

$$$$ PEDRO LARUMBE. This excellent restaurant is literally the pinnacle of the ABC shopping center between Paseo de Castellana and Calle Serrano. Dining quarters include a lovely summer roof terrace, which is glassed in for the winter, and an Andalusian patio. Chef-owner Pedro Larumbe is known for his presentations of such contemporary dishes as *cazuela de cocochas con patatas al pil-pil*, a casserole of tender cheeks of hake, cooked in their own juices combined with oil and garlic, and served with potatoes. There's a salad bar at lunchtime, and the dessert buffet is an art exhibit. Good wine list. *Castellana 34/Serrano 61, tel. 91/575–1112. AE, DC, MC, V. Closed Sun., Easter wk, and 2 wks in Aug. No lunch Sat.*

$$$ ASADOR FRONTÓN. This popular, long-established Basque restaurant serves some of the most outstanding meat and fish in Madrid. It has a few satellites now, but the original is more old-fashioned, and still has a jolly waitstaff—unusual in Spain. Appetizers include *anchoa fresca* (fresh grilled anchovies) and *pimientos rellenos con bacalao* (peppers stuffed with cod). The huge, delicious *chuleton* (T-bone steak), seared on a charcoal grill and lightly sprinkled with sea salt, is for two or more; order *cogollo de lechuga* (lettuce hearts) or another vegetable to accompany. The tender *cocochas de merluza* (hake morsels in green parsley sauce) are deliciously light. *Tirso de Molina 7 (upstairs at back), tel. 91/369–1617. Reservations essential. AE, DC, MC, V. Closed Sun.*

$$$ PARADÍS. Paradís serves avant-garde Catalan cuisine in a stylish, sophisticated setting that's ideally suited for lunch. (It's brightly lit and touristy at dinnertime.) Magret of duck lacquered with spices, an assortment of sautéed wild mushrooms, and *bacalao de Girona* (cod in the traditional style of this Catalan town) are examples of the rich fare. *Marqués de Cuba 14, tel. 91/429–7303. Reservations essential. AE, DC, V. Closed Sun. No lunch Sat.*

$$ BOTÍN. The *Guinness Book of Records* calls this the world's oldest restaurant (1725), and Hemingway called it the best. The latter claim may be a bit over the top, but the restaurant is excellent and extremely charming (and so successful that the owners opened a "branch" in Miami, Florida, in 1998). There are four floors of tiled, wood-beamed dining rooms, and if you're seated upstairs you'll pass ovens dating back several centuries. Musical groups called *tunas* often drop in to meander among the tourist hordes in traditional garb. Essential specialties are *cochinillo asado* (roast suckling pig) and *cordero asado* (roast lamb). It is said that Goya washed dishes here before he made it as a painter. *Cuchilleros 17, off Plaza Mayor, tel. 91/366–4217. AE, DC, MC, V.*

$$ CASA LASTRA. Established in 1926, this little Asturian restaurant-bar is popular with locals in the charming Lavapié district. It has a distinctly rustic feel, its half-tiled walls strung with relics from the Asturian countryside, including wooden clogs and cow bells along with sausages and garlic. Specialties include *fabada* (Asturian ham and white-bean stew), *fabas con almejas* (white beans with clams), and *queso de cabrales*, Spain's super-tangy blue cheese, made in the Picos de Europa from a mixture of milk from cows, goats, and sheep. Desserts include baked apples. Great hunks of crisp bread and hard Asturian cider can complement a hearty meal on a 2,200-pta. weekday set menu. *Olivar 3, tel. 91/369–0837. AE, MC, V. Closed Wed. and July. No dinner Sun.*

$$ CASA PACO. ★ This popular Castilian tavern wouldn't have looked out of place two or three centuries ago. Squeeze your way past the old, zinc-topped bar, always crowded with Madrileños downing shots of red wine, and into the tiled dining rooms. People come here to feast on thick slabs of red meat, served sizzling on plates so hot that the meat continues to cook at your table. The beef is superb, and the Spanish consider overcooking a sin, so be prepared for looks of dismay if you ask for your meat well done (*bien hecho*). You order by weight, so remember that a *medio kilo* is more than a pound. Try the *pisto manchego* (the La Mancha version of ratatouille) to start. *Puerta Cerrada 11, tel. 91/366–3166. DC, V. Closed Sun. and Aug.*

$$ LA BOLA. ★ First opened as a *botellería* (wine shop) in 1802, La Bola developed slowly into a tapas bar and eventually into a full-fledged restaurant. Tradition is the main draw; blood-red paneling outside beckons you into the original bar and the cozy dining nooks, decorated with polished wood, Spanish tile, and lace curtains. The restaurant still belongs to the founding family, with the seventh generation currently in training. Dinner is served, but the house specialty is that quintessential Madrid meal *cocido a la madrileña*, served only at lunch and accompanied by crusty bread and a hearty red wine. *Bola 5, tel. 91/547–6930. No credit cards. No dinner Sun.*

$$ LA CACHARRERÍA. The name of this restaurant means "junkyard," and it's reflected in the funky decor—a mix of dusty calico, old lace, and gilt mirrors, all tucked into the medieval quarter. The cooking, however, is decidedly upscale, with a market-based menu that changes daily and an excellent selection of wines. Venison stew and fresh tuna steaks with *cava* (sparkling white wine from Catalonia) and leeks have been among the specialties. Whatever else you order, save room for the homemade lemon tart. *Moreiria 9, tel. 91/365–3930. AE, DC, MC, V. Closed Sun.*

$$ LAS CUEVAS DE LUIS CANDELAS. Hidden just off the southwest corner of the Plaza Mayor, this "cave" is said to be the oldest tavern in Madrid and feels like the medieval cellar of a Spanish mansion. Popular with locals as well as travelers, the tavern is divided into three sections. You're greeted by a host dressed as the 19th-century bandit himself, and you enter through a long bar where noisy regulars drink and munch tapas. A low stone archway leads to a quieter area where you can sit on low benches, drink from a ceramic jar, and eat *raciones* of such tapas as mushrooms in garlic and cured ham. Farther inside the "cave" are the dining areas, with painted scenes of old Madrid. Barbecued meats are the specialty, and portions are huge and heavy—for a light dinner, stay in the tapas lounge. A guitar player strolls between the ancient rooms, adding to the enchanting, if slightly touristy, atmosphere. *Cuchilleros 1, tel. 91/366–5428. AE, MC, V.*

$ CASA MINGO. Resembling an Asturian cider tavern, Casa Mingo
★ is built into a stone wall beneath the Estación del Norte, across the street from the hermitage of San Antonio de la Florida. It's a bustling place; you share long plank tables with other diners, and the only items on the menu are succulent roast chicken, salad, and sausages, all to be washed down with numerous bottles of *sidra* (hard cider). Small tables are set up on the sidewalk in summer. Get here early (1 for lunch, 8:30 for dinner) if you want to avoid a wait. *Paseo de la Florida 2, tel. 91/547–7918. Reservations not accepted. No credit cards.*

$ CHAMPAGNERÍA GALA. Hidden on a back street not far from Calle Atocha and the Reina Sofía museum, this cheerful Mediterranean restaurant is usually packed thanks to its fixed-price three-course menus with wine, which offer a choice of paellas, *fideus* (paellas with noodles instead of rice), risottos, and hearty bean stews. Only *cava*, Catalan sparkling wine, costs extra. The front dining area is a kaleidoscope of painted color, particularly red; the back area incorporates trees and plants in a glassed-in patio. *Moratín 22, tel. 91/429–2562. Reservations essential. No credit cards.*

$ SANABRESA. Be prepared for bright lights, plastic plants, spotless white tablecloths, and diners glancing at the TV as they dig into classic, sensibly priced Spanish fare—hearty, wholesome meals like *pechuga villaroy* (breaded and fried chicken breast in béchamel) and, on Thursday, paella. The functional, pink-wall dining room is always crowded, so if you don't arrive early (1:30 for lunch or 8:30 for dinner), you'll probably have to wait. *Amor de Dios 12, tel. 91/429–0338. Reservations not accepted. AE, MC, V. Closed Sun. and Aug.*

VEGETARIAN

$ LA BIOTIKA. A vegetarian's dream in the heart of the bar district just east of Plaza Santa Ana, this small, cozy restaurant serves macrobiotic vegetarian cuisine seven days a week. Enormous salads, hearty soups, fresh bread, and creative tofu dishes make the meal flavorful as well as healthy. A small shop at the entrance sells macrobiotic groceries. *Amor de Dios 3, tel. 91/429–0780. No credit cards.*

In This Section

Updated by Edward Owen

shopping

MADRID HAS MORE ON OFFER than Lladró porcelain and bullfighting posters; Spain has been recognized in recent years as one of the world's top design centers. You'll have no trouble finding traditional crafts in Madrid, such as ceramics, guitars, and leather goods (albeit not at countryside prices), but don't stop there. The city is now more like Rodeo Drive than the bargain bin that it was just a decade ago. Known for contemporary furniture and decorative items as well as chic clothing, shoes, and jewelry, Spain's capital is stiff competition for Barcelona, a city that now considers itself the fashion capital of Europe. Most shops accept most major credit cards.

DEPARTMENT STORES

El Corte Inglés. Spain's largest department store carries the best selection of everything, from auto parts to groceries to designer fashions. *tel. 901/122122 for general information, tel. 902/ 400222 for ticket sales. Preciados 3, tel. 91/531–9619; Goya 76 and 87, tel. 91/432–9300; Princesa 56, tel. 91/454–6000; Serrano 47, tel. 91/432–5490; Raimundo Fernández Villaverde 79, tel. 91/418–8800.*

Marks & Spencer. British chain "Marks & Sparks" is best known for its woolens and underwear, but most shoppers head straight for the gourmet-food shop in the basement. *Serrano 52, tel. 91/ 520–0000.*

Zara. For those with young tastes and slim pocketbooks (picture hip clothes that you'll throw away in about six months), Zara has the latest looks for men, women, and children. *Centro*

Comercial ABC, Serrano 61, tel. 91/575–6334; Gran Vía 32, tel. 91/
522–9727; Princesa 63, tel. 91/543–2415; Conde de Peñalver 4, tel. 91/
435–4135.

DISTRICTS

Madrid has two main shopping areas. The first is in the center of
town, around the **Puerta del Sol,** and includes the major
department stores (El Corte Inglés, the French music-and-book
chain FNAC, etc.) and a large number of mid-range shops in the
streets nearby. The second area, far more elegant and
expensive, is in the northwestern **Salamanca** district, bounded
roughly by Serrano, Goya, and Conde de Peñalver. These
streets, just off the Plaza de Colón (particularly Calle Serrano),
have the widest selection of smart boutiques and designer
fashions—think Prada, Armani, and Donna Karan New York, as
well as renowned Spanish designers such as Sybilla and Josep
Font-Luz Diaz. If you're in the market for clothes, you may find
that Spaniards, like Italians, favor brown tones; cool palettes
don't prevail, though of course black is readily available.

Galerías del Prado (Plaza de las Cortes 7) is an attractive mall
tucked under the Palace Hotel on the Paseo del Prado. Shop
here for fine books, gourmet foods, clothing, leather goods, art,
and more. Madrid's newest mall is a four-decker: the **Centro
Comercial ABC** (Paseo de la Castellana 34/Serrano 61), named
for the daily newspaper founded on the premises in the 19th
century. The building is a beautifully restored landmark with an
ornate tile facade; inside, a large café is surrounded by shops of
all kinds, including leather stores and hairdressers. The fourth-
floor restaurant has a rooftop terrace with scenic urban views.
For street-chic shopping closer to medieval Madrid, check out
the playful window displays at the **Madrid Fusion Centro de
Moda** (Plaza Tirso de Molina 15, tel. 91/369–0018), where up-
and-coming Spanish design houses fill five floors with faux furs,
funky jewelry, and Madrid's most eccentric collection of shoes.

ONE LAST TRAVEL TIP:

Pack an easy way to reach the world.

Wherever you travel, the MCI WorldCom Card℠ is the easiest way to stay in touch. You can use it to call to and from more than 125 countries worldwide. And you can earn bonus miles every time you use your card. So go ahead, travel the world. MCI WorldCom℠ makes it even more rewarding. For additional access codes, visit **www.wcom.com/worldphone**.

MCI WORLDCOM.

EASY TO CALL WORLDWIDE

1. Just dial the WorldPhone® access number of the country you're calling from.

2. Dial or give the operator your MCI WorldCom Card number.

3. Dial or give the number you're calling.

Belgium ◆	0800-10012
Czech Republic ◆	00-42-000112
Denmark ◆	8001-0022

France ◆	0-800-99-0019
Germany	0800-888-8000
Hungary ◆	06▼-800-01411
Ireland	1-800-55-1001
Italy ◆	172-1022
Mexico	01-800-021-8000
Netherlands ◆	0800-022-91-22
Spain	900-99-0014
Switzerland ◆	0800-89-0222
United Kingdom	0800-89-0222
United States	1-800-888-8000

◆ Public phones may require deposit of coin or phone card for dial tone. ▼ Wait for second dial tone.

EARN FREQUENT FLIER MILES

Bureau de change

Cambio

外国為替

In this city, you can find money on almost any street.

NO-FEE FOREIGN EXCHANGE

The Chase Manhattan Bank has over 80 convenient
locations near New York City destinations such as:

Times Square
Rockefeller Center
Empire State Building
2 World Trade Center
United Nations Plaza

Exchange any of 75 foreign currencies

THE RIGHT RELATIONSHIP IS EVERYTHING.®

FLEA MARKET

On Sunday, Calle de Ribera de Curtidores is closed to traffic and jammed with outdoor booths selling everything under the sun—its weekly transformation into **El Rastro**. The crowds grow so thick that it takes a while just to advance a few feet amid the hawkers and the gawkers. A word of warning: pickpockets abound here. Hang on to your purse and wallet, and be especially careful if you choose to bring a camera. The flea market sprawls into most of the surrounding streets, with certain areas specializing in particular products. Many of the goods sold here are wildly overpriced.

But what goods! The Rastro has everything from antique furniture to exotic parrots and cuddly puppies; from pirated cassette tapes of flamenco music to key chains emblazoned with symbols of the CNT, Spain's old anarchist trade union. Practice your Spanish by bargaining with the vendors over paintings, colorful Gypsy oxen yokes, heraldic iron gates, new and used clothes, and even hashish pipes. They may not lower their prices, but sometimes they'll throw in a handmade bracelet or a stack of postcards to sweeten the deal.

Off the Ribera are two *galerías*, courtyards where small shops offer higher-quality, higher-priced antiques and other goods. The whole spectacle shuts down around 2 PM.

SPECIALTY STORES
Books and Maps—The Outdoors

Established in 1950, **La Tienda Verde** (Maudes 23 and 38, tel. 91/535–3810) is a paradise for outdoor enthusiasts planning hikes, mountain-climbing expeditions, spelunking trips, and so forth, with detailed maps and (Spanish-language) guidebooks.

Boutiques and Fashion

Adolfo Domínguez (Serrano 96, tel. 91/576–7053; Serrano 18, tel. 91/577–8280) is one of Spain's best-known designers, with lines for both men and women. One of Spain's premier young designers, **Jesús del Pozo** (Almirante 9, tel. 91/531–3646) also caters to both sexes. His boutique is an excellent, if pricey, place to pick up some classic Spanish style. **Seseña** (De la Cruz 23, tel. 91/531–6840) has outfitted Hollywood stars (and Hillary Rodham Clinton) and famous painters since the turn of the century, with capes in wool or velvet, some lined with red satin. **Sybilla** (Jorge Juan 12, tel. 91/578–1322) is the studio of Spain's best-known female designer. Her fluid dresses and hand-knit sweaters, which have made her a favorite with supermodel Helena Christensen, come in natural colors and fabrics.

Ceramics

Antigua Casa Talavera (Isabel la Católica 2, tel. 91/547–3417) is the best of Madrid's numerous ceramics shops. Despite the name, the finest ware sold here is from Manises, near Valencia, but the blue-and-yellow Talavera ceramics are also excellent. **Cerámica El Alfar** (Claudio Coello 112, tel. 91/411–3587) is laden with pottery from all corners of Spain. **Sagardelos** (Zurbano 46, tel. 91/310–4830) specializes in distinctive, modern Spanish ceramics from Galicia and has excellent selections of breakfast sets, coffee pots, and objets d'art.

Crafts and Design

Casa Julia (Almirante 1, tel. 91/522–0270) is an artistic showcase, with two floors of tasteful antiques, paintings by up-and-coming artists, and furniture in experimental designs. It's a great place to hunt for nontraditional souvenirs. **El Arco** (Plaza Mayor 9, tel. 91/365–2680) has a good selection of contemporary handicrafts from all over Spain, including modern ceramics, handblown glassware, jewelry, and leather items as well as a whimsical collection of pendulum clocks.

Fans

Casa Diego (Puerta del Sol 12, tel. 91/522–6643), established in 1853, stocks a classic collection of fans, umbrellas, and classic Spanish walking sticks with ornamented silver handles. The British royal family buys autograph fans here—white kidskin fans for signing on special occasions.

Food and Wine

The Club Gourmet sections in **El Corte Inglés** (☞ Department Stores, *above*) stores present a wide choice of Spanish wines, olive oils, and foodstuffs. Handily located near Plaza Santa Ana and Plaza de les Cortés, **González** (Calle Léon 21, tel. 91/429–5618) features fine Spanish wines, olive oils, cheeses, hams, dried pulses, and other foods. Sample the offerings at the wine bar at back. **Lavinina** (José Ortega y Gasset 16, tel. 91/426–0604) claims to be the largest wine store in Europe, and does have a massive selection of bottles, books, and bar accessories. The upscale chain **Mallorca** (Velázquez 59, tel. 91/431–9909; Serrano 6, tel. 91/577–1859; Centro Comercial, Goya 6, tel. 91/577–2123) sells prepared meals, cocktail canapés, chocolates, and wines, and has tapas counters for sampling.

Guitars

José Ramirez (General Margallo 10, tel. 91/571–8431) has provided Spain and the rest of the world with guitars since 1882. Prices start at 15,000 ptas. The shop includes a museum of antique instruments. **Real Música** (Carlos III 1, tel. 91/541–3007), around the corner from the Teatro Real, is a music lover's dream, with Madrid's best selection of guitars and other instruments as well as sheet music, CDs, memorabilia, and a savvy staff.

Hats

Century-old **Casa Yustas** (Plaza Mayor 30, tel. 91/366–5084) carries every type of headgear from the old three-corner, patent-leather hats of the Guardia Civil to the berets worn by the

Clothing Size Conversion Chart

Women's Clothing

US	UK	EUR
4	6	34
6	8	36
8	10	38
10	12	40
12	14	42

Women's Shoes

US	UK	EUR
5	3	36
6	4	37
7	5	38
8	6	39
9	7	40

Men's Suits

US	UK	EUR
34	34	44
36	36	46
38	38	48
40	40	50
42	42	52
44	44	54
46	46	56

Men's Shirts

US	UK	EUR
14 ½	14 ½	37
15	15	38
15 ½	15 ½	39
16	16	41
16 ½	16 ½	42
17	17	43
17 ½	17 ½	44

Men's Shoes

US	UK	EUR
7	6	39 ½
8	7	41
9	8	42
10	9	43
11	10	44 ½
12	11	46

Guardia's frequent enemy, the Basques. These berets are much wider than those worn by the French and make excellent gifts.

Leather Goods

On a street full of bargain shoe stores (*muestrarios*), **Caligae** (Augusto Figueroa 27, tel. 91/531–5343) is probably the best of the bunch. Posh **Loewe** (Serrano 26 and 34, tel. 91/577–6056; Gran Vía 8, tel. 91/532–7024; Palace Hotel, tel. 91/429–8530) features ultra–high quality designer purses, accessories, and clothing made of buttery-soft leather in dyed, jewel-like colors. Prices can hit the stratosphere. **Tenorio** (Plaza de la Provincia 6, tel. 91/366–4440) is where you'll find those fine old boots of Spanish leather, made to order with workmanship that should last a lifetime and is priced accordingly, starting at 110,000 ptas.

Toys

The charming shop **Gepetto** (Diego de León 47, tel. 91/563–4507) sells more than just puppets, particularly handcrafted wooden toys in all shapes and sizes. They're on the expensive end, but some of these pieces are works of art and make exquisite gifts for toy lovers of any age.

In This Section

Updated by Edward Owen

outdoor activities and sports

MADRILEÑOS ARE A VIGOROUS, JOYFUL LOT, famous for their ability to defy sleep. They embrace their city's vibrant sports activities with as much zest as they do its cultural opportunities and nightlife. And you need only witness a bullfight at Las Ventas or a Real Madrid soccer match at Santiago Bernabeu Stadium to see that, in some cases, culture and sport are one in the same. What's more, Spain's fair weather is ideally suited to spending time outdoors virtually year-round. In summer, however, it's best to restrict physical activity to early morning or late afternoon.

PARTICIPANT SPORTS
Golf

Golf Olivar de la Hinojosa (Avda. Dublín s/n, tel. 91/721–1889), in Campo de las Naciones outside town, is open to the public with two courses (one 18 holes, one 9) and golf lessons.

Horseback Riding

Northeast of Madrid, **Club Hipica Mirasierra** (Carretera de Fuencarral al Pardo, Km 2.2, tel. 91/747–7627) and the neighboring **Hipica Alameda del Pardo** (Carretera Fuencarral al Pardo, Km 2.3, tel. 91/372–0958) rent horses and equipment to both children and adults, with lessons and short guided treks.

Running

Your best bet is the **Parque del Retiro,** where one path circles the entire park and numerous others weave their way under trees and through formal gardens. The **Casa de Campo** is crisscrossed by numerous, sunnier trails.

Swimming

Madrid has the perfect antidote to the dry, sometimes intense heat of the summer months—a superb system of clean, popular, well-run municipal swimming pools (admission about 350 ptas.). The biggest and best—fitted with a comfortable, tree-shaded restaurant—is in the **Casa de Campo** (take the metro to Lago and walk up the hill a few yards; tel. 91/463–0050). Another good choice in the city center is the **Piscina Canal Isabel II** (Plaza Juan Zorrila, entrance off Avda. de Filipinas, no phone), with diving boards and a wading pool for kids.

Tennis

Club de Tenis Chamartín (Federico Salmon 2, tel. 91/345–2500) is open to the public with 28 courts. There are also public courts in the **Casa de Campo** and on the Avenida de Vírgen del Puerto, behind the Palacio Real. The tourist office has details.

SPECTATOR SPORTS
Bullfighting

Bullfighting is really a spectacle, not a sport. For those not turned off by the death of six bulls every Sunday afternoon from April to early November, it offers all the excitement of a major stadium event. Nowhere in the world is bullfighting better than at Madrid's **Las Ventas** (C. Alcalá 231, tel. 91/356–2200; metro: Las Ventas), formally called the Plaza de Toros Monumental. The sophisticated audience, which follows taurine matters closely, is more critical in Madrid than anywhere else, and if you're uninitiated you'll be amazed at how confusing their reactions to the fights can be. Cheers and hoots are difficult at first to distinguish, and it may take years to understand what prompts the wrath of this hard-to-please crowd. For a traveler, the bullfight audience can be the most entertaining part of the experience. Tickets can be purchased at the ring or, for a 20% surcharge, at one of the agencies on Calle Victoria, just off the Puerta del Sol. Most fights start in late afternoon, and the best fights of all—the world's top displays of bullfighting—come during the three weeks of consecutive daily fights that mark the feast of San Isidro, in May. Tickets can be tough to get through normal channels, but they're always available from scalpers in the Calle Victoria and at the stadium. You can bargain, but even Spaniards pay prices of perhaps 10 times the face value—up to 20,000 ptas. or even more.

NEED A
BREAK?
El Albero (Pedro Heredia 21, tel. 91/355–1087) is an atmospheric bullfight bar and restaurant near the bullring. Have a tapa or a meal, perhaps with *rabo de toro*, bull's-tail stew. Enthusiastic owners José and Miguel Martín have entertained *aficionados* since 1991. To find the place, cross Alcalá in front of the ring, walk up and turn left down Maestro Alonso.

Soccer

Spain's number-one sport is known locally as *fútbol*. Madrid has two teams, Real Madrid and Atlético Madrid, both among Europe's best, and two stadiums to match. The enormous **Santiago Bernabeu Stadium** (Paseo de la Castellana 140, tel. 91/398–4300), which seats 75,000, is home to the more popular Real Madrid, while the **Vicente Calderón Stadium** (Virgen del Puerto 67, tel. 91/366–4704 or 91/364–0888), on the outskirts of town, is where Atlético Madrid defends. You'll generally have to stand in line at the stadium to get tickets, but tickets for many major games are available at agencies inside Corte Inglés department stores (☞ Shopping).

In This Section

Updated by Edward Owen

nightlife and the arts

NIGHTLIFE—OR LA MARCHA, as the Spanish fondly call it—reaches legendary heights in Spain's capital. It has been said that Madrileños rarely sleep, largely because they spend so much time in bars—not drunk, but socializing in the easy, sophisticated way that's unique to this city. This is true of old as well as young, and it's not uncommon for children to play on the sidewalks past midnight while multigenerational families and friends convene over coffee or cocktails at an outdoor café. The streets best known for their social scenes, however, do tend to attract a younger clientele; these include Huertas, Moratín, Segovia, Victoria, and the areas around the Plaza Santa Ana and the Plaza de Anton Martín. The adventurous may want to explore the scruffier bar district around the Plaza Dos de Mayo, in the Malasaña area, where trendy, smoke-filled hangouts line both sides of Calle San Vicente Ferrer. Equally brave souls can venture a few blocks east to the notorious haunts of neighboring Chueca, popular with gays, where tattoo studios and street-chic boutiques break up the endless alleys of techno discos and after-hours clubs.

As Madrid's reputation as a vibrant, contemporary arts center has grown, artists and performers of all stripes have arrived in droves. The best way to stay abreast of events is to consult the weekly *Guía de Ocio* (published Monday) or daily listings in the leading newspaper, *El País*, both of which are easy to comprehend even if you don't read Spanish. Performance tickets are usually best purchased at the hall itself or, in the case of major pop concerts, at **El Corte Inglés** department stores (tel. 902/400222), **FNAC**

(Preciados 28, tel. 91/595–6100), or **Tele-Entradas** (tel. 902/101212).

The city throws major arts festivals in each of the four seasons. The most comprehensive is the Festival de Otoño (Autumn Festival), from late September to late November, which blankets the entire city with pop concerts, poetry readings, flamenco, and ballet and theater from world-renowned companies. Other annual events include world-class bonanzas of jazz, salsa, African-music, and rock; art exhibits; film festivals; and more, all at very reasonable prices. Many events take place outdoors, in city parks and stadiums.

NIGHTLIFE

Bars

Madrid has countless bars, and while almost all serve food, many are known more for their atmosphere. Some recommendations:

ALHAMBRA. This one-room tavern has been serving excellent wine, beer, and tapas to a gregarious crowd since 1929. Alhambra opens at an eye-popping 9:30 AM; around midnight it fills up, the windows get steamy, and the crowd does pseudo-*sevillana* dance moves to traditional music. When it's packed, they jump right onto the wooden tabletops without missing a beat. *Victoria 9, tel. 91/521–0708.*

CAFE GIJÓN. Possibly Madrid's most famous café-bar, the Gijón has hosted the city's most highfalutin *tertulias* (discussion groups that meet regularly to hash out the issues of the day) for more than a century. *Paseo de Recoletos 21, tel. 91/521–5425.*

EL CLANDESTINO. Run by a French couple who seem to be Spaniards at heart, this bar-café is a hidden, low-key hot spot with a local following: atmosphere without attitude. Impromptu jam sessions are rounded out by two floors alternating mellow jazz with house and ambient music. *Barquillo 34, tel. 91/521–5563.*

HARD ROCK CAFE. Wildly popular with young Spaniards, Madrid's version of the U.S. classic opened in 1994, serving up the usual drinks, burgers, and salads with a heavy dose of loud music. *Paseo Castellana 2, tel. 91/436–4340.*

LOS GABRIELES. This building is featured in most Madrid tourist literature for its remarkable tiled walls—advertisements from the turn of the 20th century, when this was a high-class brothel. Drinks are unusually pricey. *Echegaray 17, tel. 91/429–6261.*

OLIVER. Here are two bars in one: afternoons and evenings, an upstairs lounge and restaurant; late at night, a full-fledged Chueco disco in the brick-lined basement cavern. *Almirante 12, tel. 91/521–7379.*

PALACIO DE GAVIRIA. Hidden away on a tawdry commercial street between Puerta del Sol and the Royal Palace, this restored 19th-century palace was allegedly built to house one of Queen Isabel II's lovers. An exotic maze, it now offers drinks in a sophisticated setting, with a disco and frequent late-night jazz in the mirrored ballroom. *Arenal 9, tel. 91/526–6069.*

SOHO. Something of a slice of New York in the Salamanca district, Soho has an eclectic menu that includes exotic island drinks as well as Spanish variants of Tex-Mex cuisine. It's filled with rap and reggae fans. *Jorge Juan 50, tel. 91/577–8973. Closed Sun.*

TABERNA DE ANTONIO SANCHEZ. It's reputed to be the oldest bar in Madrid, and the proprietors claim it's been around since 1830. Order wine and tapas at the old zinc bar in front; head to the back for a full meal. *Mesón de Paredes 13, tel. 91/539–7826.*

VIVA MADRID. This extremely popular bar has a Brassai motif and a serious personality. Packed with both Spaniards and foreigners, it has become something of a singles scene. There are tables and a small selection of bar food in the rear. *Manuel Fernández y González 7, tel. 91/429–3640.*

Cabaret

BERLIN CABARET (Costanilla de San Pedro 11, tel. 91/366–2034) professes to provide authentic cabaret as it was performed in Berlin in the '30s. (These days the audience is quite different.) Combining magic, chorus girls, and ribald comedy, it draws an eccentric crowd for vintage café theater. On weekends, the absurd fun lasts until daybreak.

Discos

Madrid's oldest and hippest disco for wild, all-night dancing to an international music mix is **El Sol** (Calle Jardines 3, tel. 91/532–6490), open 'til 5:30 AM. There's live music around midnight Thursday, Friday, and Saturday. **Joy Eslava** (Arenal 11, tel. 91/366–3733), a downtown disco in a converted theater, is an old standby. **Pacha** (Barceló 11, tel. 91/447–0128), one of Spain's infamous chain discos, is always energetic. **Fortuny** (Fortuny 34, tel. 91/319–0588) attracts a celebrity crowd, especially in summer, when the lush outdoor patio opens for partying under the stars. Put on your best dancing shoes: the door is ultraselective. Salsa has become a fixture in Madrid; check out the most spectacular moves at **Azúcar** (Sugar; Paseo Reina Cristina 7, tel. 91/501–6107).

Flamenco

Madrid is not a great city for flamenco, but if you won't be traveling south, here are a few possibilities. Note that prices for dinner and a show tend to be very high; you can save money by dining elsewhere and arriving in time for the show. Drinks are usually extra.

CAFÉ DE CHINITAS. It's expensive, but the flamenco dancing here is the best in Madrid. Try to reserve in advance; shows often sell out. Performances are at 10:30 PM Monday through Saturday. *Torrija 7, tel. 91/559–5135.*

CASA PATAS. Along with tapas, this well-known space offers good, if somewhat touristy, flamenco. Prices are more reasonable than elsewhere. Shows are at 10:30 PM Monday–Thursday, midnight Friday–Sunday. *Canizares 10, tel. 91/369–0496.*

CORRAL DE LA MORERÍA. Dinner à la carte and well-known visiting flamenco stars accompany the resident dance troupe. Since Morería opened its doors in 1956, celebrities such as Frank Sinatra and Ava Gardner have left their autographed photos for the walls. Shows are daily, from 10:45 PM to 2 AM. *Morería 17 (on C. Bailén, cross bridge over Calle Segovia and turn right), tel. 91/365–8446.*

Nightclubs

Jazz, rock, flamenco, and classical music are all popular in Madrid's many small clubs.

AMADIS. Here, telephones on every table encourage people to call each other with invitations to dance. *Covarrubias 42 (underneath Luchana Cinema), tel. 91/446–0036.*

CAFÉ CENTRAL. Madrid's best-known jazz venue is chic and well run, and the musicians are often internationally known. Performances are usually from 10 PM to midnight. *Plaza de Ángel 10, tel. 91/369–4143.*

CAFE DEL FORO. This funky, friendly club on the edge of Malasaña has live music every night starting at 11:30 PM. *San Andrés 38, tel. 91/445–3752.*

CAFÉ JAZZ POPULART. Blues, jazz, Brazilian music, reggae, and salsa start at 11 PM. *Huertas 22, tel. 91/429–8407.*

CHOCOLATERÍA SAN GINÉS. Open from 6 PM to 7 AM, this is traditionally the last stop of the bleary-eyed after a hedonistic night out. Stumble in for great cups of thick *chocolate*, crisp *churros,* and a glass of water. *Pasadizo de San Ginés (enter by Arenal 11), tel. 91/365–6546. Closed Mon.*

CLAMORES. This famous jazz club serves a wide selection of French and Spanish champagnes. *Albuquerque 14, tel. 91/445–7938.*

NEGRA TOMASA. Under palm fronds and fishnets, the crowd drinks mojitos (made from sugar, crushed limes, mint, crushed ice, and flavored rum) to horns, maracas, and drums at this Cuban music bar. The house trio draws an international crowd on weekends. *C. Espoz y Mina and C. Cadiz,* tel. 91/523–5830.

SIROCO. The music is live until 12:30 AM Thursday to Saturday; then funk and techno reign until 6 AM. *San Dimas 3,* tel. 91/593–3070.

SURISTAN. This relaxed venue just off the Plaza Santa Ana is a café by day, a college bar by evening, and an avant-garde theater of sorts late at night. It's a hip indie spot for nightly rock and pop concerts, as well as occasional theater and readings. *La Cruz 7,* tel. 91/532–3909.

TORERO. A thoroughly modern club despite its name, Torero is for the beautiful people—quite literally: a bouncer allows only those judged *gente guapa* (beautiful people) to enter. It's one of Madrid's most stylin' spots. *Cruz 26,* tel. 91/523–1129.

Tapas Bars

A *tapa* is a bit of food that usually comes free with a drink; it might be a few olives, a mussel in vinaigrette, a sardine, or spicy potatoes. You can also order a larger plate of this kind of snack, called a *ración,* meant to be shared among friends. The practice of spending the evening wandering from bar to bar and eating tapas is so popular that the Spanish have a verb to describe it: *tapear.*

Madrid has some of the best tapas bars in Spain. The best place to start a tapa tour is near the Plaza Santa Ana or in the *mésones* built into the wall beneath the Plaza Mayor, along Cava de San Miguel. These are some of the oldest buildings in Madrid, and each bar specializes in a different tapa—for example, potato-and-egg tortillas (a Spanish tortilla is an omelet of sorts, not to be confused with the Mexican tortilla), garlicky mushrooms, or a small wedge of *empanada de atún*, a rich baked pastry stuffed with tuna, egg, and onions. Here are a few more suggestions:

BOCAÍTO. This bar is said by some to serve the best tapas in Madrid—a heady claim. *Libertad 6, tel.* 91/532–1219.

EL ABUELO. A legendary favorite even in the tapa-saturated Plaza Santa Ana area, El Abuelo (The Grandfather) serves only two tapas—and does them better than anyone else: grilled shrimp and shrimp sautéed with garlic. House tradition is to drink the sweet, red homemade house wine while tossing shrimp shells onto the floor. *Victoria 12, tel.* 91/521–2319.

EL REY DE PIMIENTO. This bar serves some 40 different kinds of tapas, including, in keeping with its name (The Pepper King), roasted red pimientos as well as the intermittently hot pimientos *de padrón. Plaza Puerta Cerrada 4, tel.* 91/365–2473.

EL VENTORRILLO. Try to come here between May and October, when tables are set up in the shady park of Las Vistillas overlooking the city's western edge. Specialties include croquettes and mushrooms. This is Madrid's best place to watch the sun go down. *C. Bailén 14, tel.* 91/366–3578.

GONZÁLEZ. Founded in 1931, González is run by Vicente Carmona, once a professor of Spanish literature in the United States. The smart, trendy deli in front sells (and will ship) the best Spanish wines, olive oils, liqueurs, hams, cheeses, cold cuts, and pastries. The paneled wine bar in back is a great place to sample the wares. *C. Léon 12, tel.* 91/429–5618.

LA CHATA. Locals frequent this stylized *castizo* tapas bar, its walls and tree-trunk beams festooned with hams, sausages, chili peppers, and bullfight photos. You get an excellent free tapa with a drink; then choose from an array of snacks on display or some great *revuelto con ajetes* (scrambled eggs with green garlic tops). A slate shows wines available by the glass. *Cava Baja 24, tel.* 91/366–1458.

LA DOLORES. Crowded and noisy, this wonderful bar is rightly reputed to serve the best draft beer in Madrid. Located just behind the Palace Hotel, it has very few tables in back. *Plaza de Jesús 4, tel. 91/429–2243.*

LA TRUCHA. Locals praise the exquisite tapas and the medieval-inn decor, hung with hams and garlic. House favorites are the enormous *plato de pescaditos fritos,* an assortment of fried fish, and *plato de ahumados,* an assortment of smoked-fish delicacies on toast. A terrace invites alfresco nibbling in summer. *Manuel Fernández y González 3, tel. 91/429–5833.*

MESÓN GALLEGO. This hole-in-the-wall serves wonderfully hearty Galician potato soup (a famous cure for those who've drunk too much) called *caldo gallego.* Not for everyone is the *Ribeiro,* the somewhat acidic white wine made with grapes from Galician riverbanks. *León 4, tel. 91/429–8997.*

MUSEO DEL JAMÓN. A small Madrid chain of tapas bars, the Ham Museum has become an institution. Look for the window full of dangling hams with hoofs. The best tapas are, of course, the air-cured hams, which come from all over the country. Don't be daunted by the variety; go for ordinary *serrano* or, if you feel like a splurge, the delicious, acorn-fed *ibérico de bellota. Carrera de San Jerónimo 6, tel. 91/458–0163; Mayor 7, tel. 91/531–4550; Paseo del Prado 44, tel. 91/420–2414.*

TABERNA DE CIEN VINOS. Popular with wine buffs on Madrid's tapas circuit, this wine bar is tucked into a charming old house with wooden shutters and stone columns. You can order a wide selection of Spanish wines by the glass, and the *raciones* border on gourmet. *Nuncio 17, tel. 91/365–4704.*

THE ARTS
Concerts/Ballet

The modern **Auditorio Nacional de Música** (Príncipe de Vergara 146, tel. 91/337–0100) is Madrid's main classical concert hall.

The newly reopened **Teatro Real** (Plaza de Isabel II, tel. 91/516–0600) is the center for ballet and opera. The new, subterranean **Centro Cultural de la Villa** (Plaza de Colón, tel. 91/575–6080 for information; 91/516–0606 for tickets) has an eclectic program ranging from gospel and blues to flamenco and Celtic dance.

Film

Nearly a dozen theaters regularly show undubbed foreign films, most in English with Spanish subtitles. These are listed in newspapers and in the *Guía de Ocio* under "V.O."—original version. Your best bet for catching an undubbed new release is the **Multicines Ideal** (Doctor Cortezo 6, tel. 91/369–2518), where half of the nine theaters are usually showing English-language art films. Other leading V.O. theaters include **Alphaville** (Martín de los Heros 14, tel. 91/584–4524) and **Renoir** (Martín de los Heros 12, tel. 91/541–4100), both just off the Plaza de España. Excellent, classic V.O. films change daily at the **Filmoteca Cine Doré** (Santa Isabel 3, tel. 91/369–1125).

Theater

English-language plays are rare. When they do come to town, they're staged at any of a dozen venues; check local newspapers. One theater you won't need Spanish for is the **Teatro de la Zarzuela** (Jovellanos 4, tel. 91/524–5400), which specializes in the traditional Spanish operetta known as *zarzuela*, a kind of bawdy comedy. The **Teatro Español** (Príncipe 25, tel. 91/429–6297) keeps 17th-century Spanish classics alive.

In This Section

Updated by Edward Owen

side trips

MADRID'S SOPHISTICATION stands in vivid contrast to the ancient ways of the historic towns nearby. Less than an hour from downtown are villages whose farm fields may still be plowed by mules. Like urbanites the world over, Madrileños chill out in the countryside, so getaways to the dozens of Castilian hamlets nearby are cherished by travelers and locals alike.

Black numbers in the margins correspond to black numbers on the Side Trips from Madrid map.

EL ESCORIAL

❶ 50 km (31 mi) northwest of Madrid.

Felipe II was one of history's most deeply religious and forbidding monarchs—not to mention one of its most powerful—and the great granite monastery that he had constructed in a remarkable 21 years (1563–84) is an enduring testament to his character. Outside Madrid in the foothills of the Sierra de Guadarrama, the **Real Monasterio de San Lorenzo de El Escorial** (Royal Monastery of St. Lawrence of Escorial) is severe, rectilinear, and unforgiving—one of the most gigantic yet simple architectural monuments on the Iberian Peninsula.

Felipe built the monastery in the village of San Lorenzo de El Escorial to commemorate Spain's crushing victory over the French at Saint-Quentin on August 10, 1557, and as a final resting place for his all-powerful father, the Holy Roman Emperor Carlos V. He filled the place with treasures as he ruled the largest empire the world has ever seen, knowing all the

while that a marble coffin awaited him in the pantheon deep below. The building's vast rectangle, encompassing 16 courts, is modeled on the red-hot grille upon which St. Lawrence was martyred—appropriate enough, since August 10 was that saint's day. (It's also said that Felipe's troops accidentally destroyed a church dedicated to St. Lawrence during the battle, and he sought to make amends.) Some years ago a Spanish psychohistorian theorized that the building is shaped like a prone woman and is thus an unintended emblem of Felipe's sexual repression. Lo and behold, this thesis provoked several newspaper articles and a rash of other commentary.

El Escorial is easily reached by car, train, bus, or organized tour; simply inquire at a travel agency or the appropriate station. Although the building and its adjuncts—a palace, museum, church, and more—can take hours or even days to tour, you should be able to include a day trip to the Valley of the Fallen, an underground basilica where General Franco is buried. Be prepared for the mobs of tourists who visit El Escorial daily, especially in summer. Midnight mass on Easter Sunday, which includes a candlelight ceremony, also draws a big crowd, so arrive at least half an hour early if you want a seat.

The monastery was begun by Juan Bautista de Toledo but finished in 1584 by Juan de Herrera, who would eventually give his name to a major Spanish architectural school. It was completed just in time for Felipe to die here, gangrenous and tortured by the gout that had plagued him for years, in the tiny, sparsely furnished bedroom that resembled a monk's cell more than the resting place of a great monarch. It is in this bedroom—which looks out, through a private entrance, into the royal chapel—that one most appreciates the man's spartan nature. Spain's later, Bourbon kings, such as Carlos III and Carlos IV, had clearly different tastes, and their apartments, connected to Felipe's by the Hall of Battles, are far more luxurious.

Perhaps the most interesting part of the entire Escorial is the **Panteón de los Reyes** (Royal Pantheon), which contains the body of every king since Carlos I save three—Felipe V (buried at La Granja), Ferdinand VI (in Madrid), and Amadeus of Savoy (in Italy). The body of Alfonso XIII, who died in Rome in 1941, was brought to El Escorial in January 1980. The rulers' bodies lie in 26 sumptuous marble and bronze sarcophagi that line the walls (three of which are empty, awaiting future rulers). Only those queens who bore sons later crowned lie in the same crypt; the

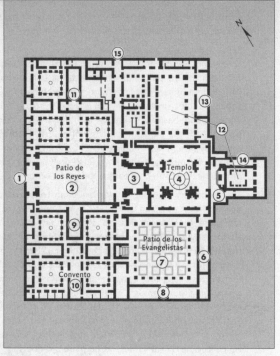

Apartments of Philip II, 14

Basilica, 4

Biblioteca (Library), 9

Choir, 3

Colegio, 11

Convent, 10

Main Entrance, 1

Museum, 13

Patio de los Evangelistas (Court of the Evangelists), 7

Patio de los Reyes (Court of the Kings), 2

Royal Palace, 12

Sacristy, 6

Salas Capitulares (Chapter Houses), 8

Stairway to Panteón de los Reyes (Royal Pantheon), 5

Tour Entrance, 15

others, along with royal sons and daughters who never ruled, lie nearby, in the **Panteón de los Infantes**. Many of the royal children are in a single circular tomb made of Carrara marble.

Another highlight is the monastery's uncharacteristically lavish and beautiful **library**, with 50,000 rare manuscripts, codices, and ancient books, including the diary of St. Teresa of Ávila and the gold-lettered, illuminated *Codex Aureus*. Tapestries, woven from cartoons by Goya, Rubens, and El Greco, cover almost every inch of wall space in huge sections of the building, and extraordinary canvases by Velázquez, El Greco, David, Ribera, Tintoretto, Rubens, and other masters have been collected from around the monastery and are now displayed in the New Museums. In the **basilica**, don't miss the fresco above the choir, depicting heaven, or Titian's fresco *The Martyrdom of St. Lawrence*, which shows the saint being roasted alive. *San Lorenzo de El Escorial, tel. 91/890–5905. 800 ptas. Apr.–Sept., Tues.–Sun. 10–6; Oct.–Mar., Tues.–Sun. 10–5.*

NEED A **BREAK?** Many Madrileños find El Escorial the perfect place for an enormous weekend lunch. Topping the list of eating spots is the outdoor terrace at **Charoles** (Floridablanca 24, tel. 91/890–5975), where imaginative seasonal specialties round out a menu of northern-Spanish favorites, such as *bacalao al pil-pil* (salt cod cooked in oil and garlic at a low temperature) and grilled *chuleta* (steak). Just don't expect picnic prices.

VALLE DE LOS CAÍDOS

❷ *13 km (8 mi) north of El Escorial on C600.*

The Valley of the Fallen is just a few minutes north of El Escorial. You drive through a pine-studded state park to this massive basilica, which is carved out of a hill of solid granite and commands magnificent views to the east. Topped with a cross nearly 500 ft high (accessible by elevator), the basilica holds the tombs of both General Franco and José Antonio Primo de Rivera, founder of the Spanish Falange. It was built with the forced labor of Republican prisoners after the civil war and dedicated, rather disingenuously, to all who died in the three-year conflict. The inside recalls *The Wizard of Oz* more than anything else, with every footstep resounding loudly off its stone walls. Tapestries of the Apocalypse add to the generally terrifying air. It's an eerie place for the midnight mass held here on Easter Sunday; the granite peak becomes truly awesome when lit by candlelight. *tel. 91/890–5611. Basilica 650 ptas., funicular 350 ptas. Apr.–Sept., Tues.–Sun. 10–7; Oct.–Mar., Tues.–Sun. 10–6.*

CHINCHÓN

③ *54 km (33 mi) southeast of Madrid, off the N III highway to Valencia on the C300 local road.*

A true Castilian town, the picturesque village of Chinchón seems a good four centuries removed. It makes an ideal day trip, especially if you save time for lunch at one of its many rustic restaurants; the only problem is that swarms of Madrileños have the same idea, so it's often hard to get a table at lunchtime on weekends.

The high point of Chinchón is its charming **Plaza Mayor**, an uneven circle of ancient three- and four-story houses embellished with wooden balconies resting on granite columns. It's something like an open-air Elizabethan theater, but with a Spanish flavor. In fact, the entire plaza is converted to a bullring from time to time, with temporary bleachers erected in the center and seats on the privately owned balconies rented out for splendid views of the festivities. (These fights are rare and tickets hard to come by, as they're snatched up by traveling Spaniards as soon as they go on sale.) The commanding **Iglesia de la Asunción** (Church of the Assumption), overlooking the plaza, is known for its Goya mural, *The Assumption of the Virgin.*

NEED A **BREAK?** On winter weekends, city dwellers reserve in droves for the superb cocido at the **Parador de Chinchón** (Avda. Generalísimo 1, tel. 91/894–0836). Two other popular restaurants on

Chinchón's arcaded plaza are **Mesón de la Virreina** (Plaza Mayor 28, tel. 91/894–0015) and **Café de la Iberia** (Plaza Mayor 17, tel. 91/894–0998), both of which have balconies for outdoor dining in season, though you may have to call ahead for such a table. The food in both is hearty Castilian fare, such as roast lamb, suckling pig, and thick steaks. Be sure to try the locally made *anís* (anise), a licorice-flavored spirit—Chinchón is so famous for its anís that Spaniards converge here every April for the annual Fiesta del Anís y del Vino (Anise and Wine Festival).

On the way back to Madrid, where C300 joins the main highway, you'll pass through the Jarama Valley. This was the scene of one of the bloodiest battles in which the Abraham Lincoln Brigade (American volunteers fighting with the Republicans against Franco in the Spanish Civil War) played a major role. The fight was immortalized by folk singer Pete Seeger, who sang, "There's a valley in Spain called Jarama . . ." Until just a few years ago, you could find bones and rusty military hardware in the fields here, and there are still a number of clearly discernible trenches.

MONASTERIO DE EL PAULAR AND LOZOYA VALLEY

④ *100 km (62 mi) north of Madrid.*

Behind the great *meseta* on which Madrid stands, the Sierra de Guadarrama rises like a dark, jagged shield separating Old and New Castile. Snowcapped for much of the year, the mountains are indeed rough-hewn in many spots, particularly on their northern face, but there is a dramatic exception—the Lozoya Valley.

About 100 km (62 mi) north of the capital, this valley of pines, poplars, and babbling brooks is a cool, green retreat from the often searing heat of the plain. Madrileños repair here for a picnic or a simple drive, rarely joined by foreign travelers, to whom the area is virtually unknown.

You'll need a car to make this trip, and the drive is a pleasant one. Take the A6 northwest from Madrid and exit at signs for the Navacerrada Pass on the N601. As you climb toward the 6,100-ft mountain pass, you'll come to a road bearing off to the left toward Cercedilla. (This little village, a popular base for hikes, is also accessible by train.) Just above Cercedilla, an old Roman road leads up to the ridge of the Guadarrama, where an ancient fountain, known as Fuenfría, long provided the spring water that fed the Roman aqueduct of Segovia. The path traced by this cobble road is very close to the route Hemingway had his hero Robert Jordan take in *For Whom the Bell Tolls*, and eventually takes you near the bridge that Jordan blew up in the novel.

If you continue past the Cercedilla road, you'll come to a ski resort at the highest point of the Navacerrada Pass. Take a right here on C604 and you'll follow the ridge of the mountains for a few miles before descending into the **Lozoya Valley.**

Looming on your left as you approach the valley floor is the **Monasterio de El Paular** (tel. 91/869–1425). Built by King Juan I in 1390, this was the first Carthusian monastery in Castile, but it has been badly neglected since the Disentailment of 1836, when religious organizations gave their artistic treasures to the state. Fewer than a dozen Benedictine monks still live here, eating and praying exactly as their predecessors did centuries ago. One of them gives daily tours every day but Thursday at noon, 1, and 5.

The monastery is attached to the hotel **Santa María de El Paular** (tel. 91/869–1011, fax 91/869–1006), most of whose rooms were tastefully refurbished in 1996. The hotel is charming but not as grand as similarly priced paradors.

The valley is filled with picnic spots along the Lozoya River, including several campgrounds. To end the excursion, take C604 north a few miles to Rascafria, and then turn right on a smaller road marked for Miraflores de la Sierra. In that town you'll turn right again, following signs for Colmenar Viejo, and then pick up a short expressway back to Madrid.

Smart Sightseeings

Savvy travelers and others who take their sightseeing seriously have skills worth knowing about.

DON'T PLAN YOUR VISIT IN YOUR HOTEL ROOM Don't wait until you pull into town to decide how to spend your days. It's inevitable that there will be much more to see and do than you'll have time for: choose sights in advance.

ORGANIZE YOUR TOURING Note the places that most interest you on a map, and visit places that are near each other during the same morning or afternoon.

START THE DAY WELL EQUIPPED Leave your hotel in the morning with everything you need for the day—maps, medicines, extra film, your guidebook, rain gear, and another layer of clothing in case the weather turns cooler.

TOUR MUSEUMS EARLY If you're there when the doors open you'll have an intimate experience of the collection.

EASY DOES IT See museums in the mornings, when you're fresh, and visit sit-down attractions later on. Take breaks before you need them.

STRIKE UP A CONVERSATION Only curmudgeons don't respond to a smile and a polite request for information. Most people appreciate your interest in their home town. And your conversations may end up being your most vivid memories.

GET LOST When you do, you never know what you'll find—but you can count on it being memorable. Use your guidebook to help you get back on track. Build wandering-around time into every day.

QUIT BEFORE YOU'RE TIRED There's no point in seeing that one extra sight if you're too exhausted to enjoy it.

TAKE YOUR MOTHER'S ADVICE Go to the bathroom when you have the chance. You never know what lies ahead.

In This Section

Updated by Edward Owen

where to stay

SPAIN'S MAJOR PRIVATE HOTEL GROUPS include the Tryp and the NH chain, which is concentrated in major cities like Madrid and which appeals to business travelers. In addition, reasonably priced hostales are concentrated in the old city between the Prado and the Puerta del Sol; start your quest around the Plaza Santa Ana. Because they're often full and don't take reservations, we list only a few here—you simply have to go door-to-door and trust your luck.

The Spanish government rates hotels with one to five stars. While quality is a factor, the rating is technically only an indication of how many facilities the hotel offers. For example, a three-star hotel may be just as comfortable as a four-star hotel but lack a swimming pool.

All hotel entrances are marked with a blue plaque bearing the letter H and the number of stars. The letter R (standing for *residencia*) after the letter H indicates an establishment with no meal service. The designations *fonda* (F), *pensión* (P), *hostal* (Hs), and *casa de huéspedes* (CH) indicate budget accommodations.

Although a single room (*habitación sencilla*) is usually available, singles are often on the small side. Solo travelers might prefer to pay a bit extra for single occupancy of a double room (*habitación doble uso individual*). All hotels we review have private bathrooms unless otherwise noted.

Prices

Prices in Madrid are about the same as those in other European capitals. The Ritz, the Palace, and the Villamagna charge upwards of U.S. $400 a night. If that's too steep, try bargaining: because most hotels cater to business travelers, special weekend rates are widely available. You may be able to save 30% on a Friday, Saturday, or Sunday night, and many hotels throw in extras, like meals or museum admissions. Business travelers on long stays can ask for discounts, which can be as deep as 40%. If you're willing to hunt a bit, you can find hostales for 4,000 ptas. or even less. Most of these very cheap rooms are on the upper floors of apartment buildings and share bath facilities.

By law, hotel prices must be posted at the reception desk and should indicate whether or not the value-added tax (IVA; 7%) is included. Breakfast is normally *not* included. Note that high-season rates prevail not only in summer but also during Holy Week and local fiestas.

CATEGORY	COST*
$$$$	over 25,000 ptas.
$$$	14,000–25,000 ptas.
$$	10,000–14,000 ptas.
$	under 10,000 ptas.

*for a standard double room, excluding tax.

$$$$ **RITZ.** When Alfonso XIII was preparing for his marriage to Queen Victoria's granddaughter, he realized to his dismay that Madrid did not have a single hotel up to the exacting standards of his royal guests. Thus was born the Ritz, and it was long the most exclusive hotel in Spain. Opened in 1910 by the king himself (who had personally overseen its construction), the Ritz is a monument to the Belle Epoque, its sumptuous public salons furnished with rare antiques, hand-embroidered linens from Robinson & Cleaver, and handwoven carpets. Guest rooms are carpeted, hung with

When it Comes to Getting Local Currency at an ATM, Same Thing.

Whether you're in Yosemite or Yemen, using your Visa® card or ATM card with the PLUS symbol is the easiest and most convenient way to get local currency. For example, let's say you're in France. When you make a withdrawal, using your secured PIN, it's dispensed in francs, but is debited from your account in U.S. dollars. This makes it easy to take advantage of favorable exchange rates. And if you need help finding one of Visa's 627,000 ATMs in 127 countries worldwide, visit **visa.com/pd/atm**. We'll make finding an ATM as easy as finding the Eiffel Tower, the Pyramids or even the Grand Canyon.

It's Everywhere You Want To Be®

SEE THE WORLD
IN FULL COLOR

Fodor's Exploring Guides bring all the great sights vividly to life with hundreds of photographs, fascinating historical background, and colorful anecdotes. Detailed maps and practical information keep you headed in the right direction.

Pair a Fodor's Exploring Guide with your trusted Fodor's Pocket Guide for a complete planning package.

Fodor's EXPLORING GUIDES

At bookstores everywhere.

chandeliers, and decorated in pastels, and many have good views of the Prado or the Castellana. Even if you can't stay here, try to visit the garden terrace for a meal: the restaurant, Goya, is justly famous (though very pricey), and Sunday brunch is a lavish affair to the soothing strains of harp music. Weekend tea and supper are accompanied by chamber music from February to May. Alas, because the lobby and lounge are often crowded with conventioneers and partygoers, the Ritz has lost much of its exclusivity. *Plaza de Lealtad 5, 28014, tel. 91/521–2857, fax 91/701–6776. 158 rooms. Restaurant, bar, in-room data ports, in-room faxes, in-room VCRs, beauty salon, massage, sauna, health club, parking (fee). AE, DC, MC, V.*

$$$$ **★ SANTO MAURO.** Once the Canadian embassy, this turn-of-the-20th-century mansion is now an intimate luxury hotel, an oasis of calm just a 10-minute cab ride from the city center. The neoclassical architecture is accented by contemporary furniture (such as suede armchairs) in such hues as mustard, teal, and eggplant. The best rooms are in the main building, as is the top-notch restaurant, which has a contemporary menu and, in season, a delightful dining terrace. Rooms in the new annex are duplexes with stereos and VCRs. Views vary; request a room with a terrace overlooking the gardens. *Zurbano 36, 28010, tel. 91/319–6900, fax 91/308–5477. 37 rooms. Restaurant, bar, coffee shop, in-room VCRs, pool, sauna, exercise room, meeting rooms, parking (fee). AE, DC, MC, V.*

$$$$ VILLA MAGNA. Part of the Park Hyatt group, the Villa Magna is one of Madrid's top luxury hotels, its concrete facade belying an exquisite interior furnished with 18th-century antiques. Prices are somewhat excessive, but it's hard to find such finishing touches as a champagne bar and—in the largest suite in Madrid—a white baby-grand piano. All rooms have large desks as well as VCRs, and all bathrooms have fresh flowers. One restaurant, Le Divellec, has cozy walnut paneling and the feel of an English library, and you can dine on its garden terrace in season. The other restaurant, the Tse-Yang, is Madrid's most exclusive for Chinese

madrid lodging

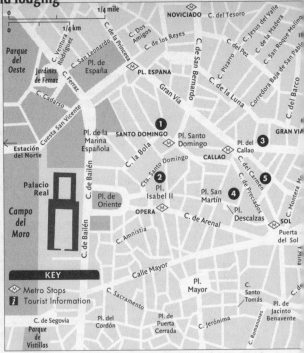

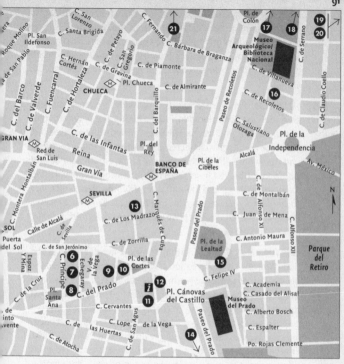

food. The hotel has direct access to a branch of El Corte Inglés department store. *Paseo de la Castellana 22, 28046, tel. 91/587–1234, fax 91/431–2286 or 91/575–3158. 164 rooms, 18 suites. 2 restaurants, 2 bars, in-room VCRs, barbershop, beauty salon, massage, sauna, health club, baby-sitting, business services, car rental, parking (fee).* AE, DC, MC, V.

$$$$ **VILLA REAL.** For a luxury hotel that combines elegance, modern amenities, and a great location, look no further. The simulated 19th-century facade gives way to lobbies garnished with potted palms. Each room has its own character, albeit with an overall French feel, and many are split-level; some suites have both saunas and whirlpool baths. The hotel faces the Cortés and is convenient to almost everything, and the staff is very friendly. *Plaza de las Cortés 10, 28014, tel. 91/420–3767, fax 91/420–2547. 94 rooms, 20 suites. Restaurant, bar, in-room data ports, beauty salon, sauna, meeting rooms, parking (fee).* AE, DC, MC, V.

$$$$ ★ **WESTIN PALACE.** Built in 1912, Madrid's most famous grand hotel is a Belle Epoque creation of Alfonso XIII and has hosted the likes of Dalí, Brando, Hayworth, and Madonna. In 1995 the hotel was acquired by Sheraton, and by 1998 it had undergone its first restoration in 85 years. Guest rooms now meet today's highest standards; banquet halls and lobbies have been lovingly beautified; and the facade has been finely restored. The Palace is more charming and stylish than ever—and while the stained-glass dome over the lounge remains exquisitely original, the windows in the guest rooms are now double glazed. The suites are no less luxurious than the opulent public spaces, and bathrooms are spacious, with double sinks, tubs, separate shower stalls, and other welcome touches such as bathrobes and magnifying mirrors. *Plaza de las Cortes 7, 28014, tel. 91/360–8000, fax 91/360–8100. 465 rooms, 45 suites. 2 restaurants, bar, café, in-room data ports, sauna, exercise room, business services, meeting rooms, parking (fee).* AE, DC, MC, V. *www.palacemadrid.com*

$$$ EL PRADO. Wedged between the classic buildings of *castizo* Madrid, this skinny new hotel is within stumbling distance of the city's best bars and nightclubs and is priced accordingly. Rooms are basic but spacious, and virtually immune to street noise thanks to double-pane windows. Decorative touches include pastel floral prints and gleaming marble baths. *C. Prado 11, 28014, tel. 91/369–0234, fax 91/429–2829. 47 rooms. Cafeteria, meeting rooms, parking (fee). AE, DC, MC, V.*

$$$ JARDÍN DE RECOLETOS. This sleek apartment hotel offers great
★ value for the money in a quiet street close to Plaza Colón and upmarket Calle Serrano. The large lobby has marble floors and a stained-glass ceiling, and adjoins a café and restaurant where you can dine or just have drinks beside a pleasant tree-lined patio. The commodious rooms, decorated with light-wood trim, white walls, and beige and yellow furnishings, include sitting and dining areas and discreet, well-equipped kitchens. "Superior" rooms and two-room suites have hydromassage baths and large terraces. Book well in advance. *Gil de Santivañes 6, 28001, tel. 91/ 781–1640, fax 91/781–1641. 36 rooms, 7 suites. Restaurant, café, in-room data ports, in-room VCRs, kitchenettes, parking (fee). AE, DC, MC, V.*

$$$ LIABENY. A large, paneled lobby leads to bars, a restaurant, and a café in this 1960s hotel, centrally located near an airy plaza (and several department stores) between Gran Vía and Puerta del Sol. The large, comfortable rooms have floral fabrics and big windows; interior and top-floor rooms are the quietest. *Salud 3, 28013, tel. 91/531–9000, fax 91/532–5306. 222 rooms. Restaurant, café, 2 bars, meeting rooms, parking (fee). AE, DC, MC, V.*

$$$ NH LAGASCA. In the heart of the elegant Salamanca neighborhood, this newish hotel combines large, brightly decorated rooms with an unbeatable location two blocks from Madrid's main shopping street, Calle Serrano. The marble lobbies border on the coldly functional, but they're fine as a meeting place. *Lagasca 64, 28001,* tel. 91/575–4606, fax 91/575–1694. 100 rooms. Restaurant, bar, in-room VCRs, meeting rooms, parking (fee). AE, DC, MC, V.

$$$ SANTO DOMINGO. An intimate hotel that artfully blends the best of classical and modern design, the Santo Domingo is about 10 minutes' walk from the Puerta del Sol, just off Gran Vía. Rooms are decorated in soft tones of peach and ocher, and those on the fifth floor have excellent views of the Royal Palace. All have voice mail and double-paned windows. An especially friendly and well trained staff gives the place a personal touch. *Plaza Santo Domingo 13, 28013, tel. 91/547–9800, fax 91/547–5995. 120 rooms. Restaurant, bar, meeting rooms, parking (fee). AE, DC, MC, V.*

$$$ SUECIA. The Suecia's chief attraction is its location, right next to the super-chic Círculo de Bellas Artes (an arts society–café–film–theater complex). The large lobby, which includes a café, is often bustling. Guest rooms are trendy, with contemporary art and futuristic light fixtures, but a little worn. *Marqués de Riera 4, 28014, tel. 91/531–6900, fax 91/521–7141. 119 rooms, 9 suites. 2 restaurants, bar, baby-sitting, parking (fee). AE, DC, MC, V.*

$$$ SUITE PRADO. Popular with Americans on short stays, this stylish apartment hotel is near the Prado, the Thyssen-Bornemisza, and the Plaza Santa Ana tapas area. The attractive attic studios on the fifth floor have sloping, beamed ceilings, and there are larger suites downstairs. All apartments are brightly decorated and have marble baths and basic kitchens, but breakfast is served by the friendly staff on weekends. *Manuel Fernández y González 10, 28014, tel. 91/420–2318, fax 91/420–0559. 18 suites. Kitchenettes, parking (fee). AE, DC, MC, V.*

$$$ TRYP AMBASSADOR. Ideally located on an old street between Gran ★ Vía and the Royal Palace, the Ambassador occupies the renovated 19th-century palace of the Dukes of Granada. A magnificent front door and a graceful three-story staircase are legacies of the building's aristocratic past; the rest has been transformed into elegant, somewhat soulless lodgings favored by executives. Guest rooms are large, complete with sitting areas, and have mahogany furnishings, floral drapes, and bedspreads. The greenhouse restaurant, filled with plants and songbirds, is especially pleasant on cold days. *Cuesta Santo Domingo 5 and 7, 28013, tel. 91/541–6700, fax 91/559–1040. 181 rooms. Restaurant, bar, airport shuttle, parking (fee). AE, DC, MC, V. www.tryp.es*

$$$ TRYP FÉNIX. A magnificent marble lobby greets your arrival at this Madrid institution, overlooking Plaza de Colón on the Castellana. The Fenix is also a mere hop from the posh shops of Calle Serrano. Its spacious rooms, decorated in reds and golds, are carpeted and amply furnished, and flowers abound. Ask for a room facing the Plaza de Colón; otherwise, the view is rather dreary. *Hermosilla 2, 28001, tel. 91/431–6700, fax 91/576–0661. 213 rooms, 12 suites. Bar, café, beauty salon, baby-sitting, parking (fee). AE, DC, MC, V.*

$$ ATLÁNTICO. Don't be put off by the location, on a noisy stretch of Gran Vía, or by the small entrance hall: the Atlántico delivers bright, clean accommodations at good prices. Rooms are small but comfortable, with fresh new furnishings. All have tile bathrooms. A member of the Best Western chain, this hotel is a favorite with anglophone travelers and is almost always full, so it's wise to book well in advance. The best layouts and views come with room numbers ending in 3, 4, or 5. *Gran Vía 38, 28013, tel. 91/522–6480, fax 91/531–0210. 80 rooms. Snack bar, airport shuttle. AE, DC, MC, V.*

$$ CARLOS V. If you like to be in the center of things, hang your hat at this classic hotel on a pedestrian street: it's mere steps from the Puerta del Sol, Plaza Mayor, and Descalzas Reales convent, and the price is right. A suit of armor decorates the tiny lobby, while crystal chandeliers add elegance to the second-floor guest lounge. All rooms are bright and carpeted, and the doubles with large terraces are a bargain. *Maestro Victoria 5, 28013, tel. 91/531–4100, fax 91/531–3761. 67 rooms, 41 with bath. Bar, airport shuttle. AE, DC, MC, V.*

$$ INGLÉS. Virginia Woolf was among the first luminaries to discover this place, which is smack in the middle of the old city's bar-and-restaurant district. Since Woolf's time, the Inglés has attracted more than its share of less-celebrated artists and writers. Rather drab and deteriorated now, it's best for those looking for location and value rather than luxury. (Run-down suites cost what you'd normally pay for a standard double.) The balconies overlooking Calle Echegaray give you an unusual aerial view of the medieval quarter, all red Mediterranean tiles and ramshackle gables. *Echegaray 8, 28014, tel. 91/429-6551, fax 91/420-2423. 58 rooms. Bar, cafeteria, exercise room, parking (fee). AE, DC, MC, V.*

$ HOSTAL DULCINEA. Run by an elderly Spanish couple (who also own the Hostal Corbero, across the street), the Dulcinea is a friendly, clean, and affordable alternative to the pricey hotels on Paseo del Prado. Just off the Plaza Cánovas del Castillo, this upper-floor pension has an arguably ideal location: it's surrounded by the Museo Thyssen-Bornemisza to the north, the Prado to the east, and the vibrant nightlife around the Plaza Santa Ana to the west. Rooms are spare, with wood furniture and minimal trimmings, but comfortable and homey. Calling ahead can get you a great price on one of the three cozy "apartments." *Cervantes 19, 28014, tel. 91/429-9309, fax 91/369-2569. 23 rooms, 3 apartments. AE, MC, V.*

$ HOSTAL VILLAR. Run by the same family for 40 years, Villar is on the second floor of a beautiful old building with a marble foyer and winding staircase. The rooms are pleasant, clean, and furnished with antique (some say "old") beds and armoires, but the real attractions are the eight rooms with balconies. These overlook lively Calle Príncipe and have corner views of the Plaza Santa Ana, including the well-heeled crowds arriving at the Teatro Español. Not all rooms are air-conditioned, and the clientele can be noisy. *Calle Príncipe 18, 28014, tel. 91/531-6600 fax 91/521-5073. 34 rooms, 18 with bath. MC, V.*

$ MORA. ★ Directly across the Paseo del Prado from the Botanical Garden, the Mora welcomes weary travelers with a sparkling, faux-marble lobby and bright, carpeted hallways. Guest rooms are modestly decorated but large and comfortable; those on the street side have great views of the gardens and the Prado, and double-paned windows keep them fairly quiet. For breakfast and lunch, the attached café is excellent, affordable, and popular with locals. *Paseo del Prado 32, 28014, tel. 91/420–1569, fax 91/420–0564. 61 rooms. Café. AE, DC, MC, V.*

$ RAMÓN DE LA CRUZ. If you don't mind a 10-minute metro ride (to Manuel Becerra) from the city center, this medium-size hotel is a find. The rooms are large, with modern bathrooms, and the stone-floor lobby is spacious. For Madrid, it's a bargain. *Don Ramón de la Cruz 94, 28006, tel. 91/401–7200, fax 91/402–2126. 103 rooms. Cafeteria. MC, V.*

PRACTICAL INFORMATION

Air Travel

There are numerous daily flights within Spain. Regular nonstop flights serve Spain from the eastern United States; flying from other North American cities usually involves a stop.

Flights from the United Kingdom to Spain are more frequent, cover small cities as well as large ones, and are priced very competitively. If you're coming from North America and would like to land in a city other than Madrid; just know that you may have to stay overnight in London or another European city on your way home. There are no direct flights to Spain from Australia or New Zealand.

BOOKING
When you book, **look for nonstop flights** and **remember that "direct" flights stop at least once.** Try to avoid connecting flights, which require a change of plane.

CARRIERS
From North America, Air Europa, American, Delta, Continental, Iberia, Spanair, TWA, and US Airways fly to Madrid. Within Spain, Iberia is the main domestic airline; two independent airlines, Air Europa and Spanair, fly a number of domestic routes at lower prices.

The Spanish predilection for cigarettes notwithstanding, most airlines serving the country, including Iberia, do not allow smoking on either international or domestic flights.

➤ FROM NORTH AMERICA: **Air Europa** (tel. 888/238–7672). **American** (tel. 800/433–7300). **Continental** (tel. 800/231–0856). **Delta** (tel. 800/221–1212). **Iberia** (tel. 800/772–4642). **Spanair** (tel. 888/545–5757). **TWA** (tel. 800/892–4141). **US Airways** (tel. 800/622–1015).

➤ FROM THE U.K.: **British Airways** (tel. 0345/222–111). **Iberia** (tel. 0207/830–0011).

➤ **WITHIN SPAIN: Iberia** (902/400500). **Air Europa** (tel. 902/401501). **Spanair** (tel. 902/131415).

CUTTING COSTS

The cheapest airfares to Spain must usually be purchased in advance and are non-refundable. Call a number of airlines, and **when you're quoted a good price, book it on the spot**—the same fare may not be available the next day. Always **check different routings** or look into using different airports. Travel agents, especially low-fare specialists (☞ Discounts & Deals, *below*), can be helpful.

Consolidators are another good source: they buy tickets for scheduled international flights at reduced rates from the airlines, then sell them at prices that beat the best fare available directly from the airlines, usually without restrictions. Sometimes you can even get your money back if you need to return the ticket. Carefully read the fine print detailing penalties for changes and cancellations, and **confirm your consolidator reservation with the airline.**

➤ **CONSOLIDATORS: Cheap Tickets** (tel. 800/377–1000). **Discount Airline Ticket Service** (tel. 800/576–1600). **Unitravel** (tel. 800/325–2222). **Up & Away Travel** (tel. 212/889–2345). **World Travel Network** (tel. 800/409–6753).

➤ **DISCOUNT PASSES:** If you buy a round-trip transatlantic ticket on Iberia, you might want to purchase a Visit Spain pass, good for four domestic flights during your trip. The pass must be purchased before you arrive in Spain, all flights must be booked in advance, and the cost is $260 ($350 if you want to include flights to the Canary Islands). Prices are $20–$50 less if you travel between October 1 and June 14.

On certain days of the week, Iberia also offers *minitarifas* (minifares), which can save you 40% on domestic flights. Tickets must be purchased in advance, and you must stay over Saturday night (☞ Discounts and Deals, *below*).

FLYING TIMES

Flying time from New York is seven hours; from London, just over two hours.

HOW TO COMPLAIN

If your baggage goes astray or your flight goes awry, complain right away. Most carriers require that you **file a claim immediately**.

Airport

Madrid is served by Barajas Airport, 12 km (7 mi) east of the city. Europe's longest runway opened for traffic here in 1999. Several major airlines have regular flights from the United States, and others serve London and other European capitals daily.

➤ AIRPORT INFORMATION: **Madrid: Barajas** (tel. 91/305–8343). **Barcelona: El Prat de Llobregat** (tel. 93/298–3838).

BETWEEN THE AIRPORT AND DOWNTOWN

Taxis wait outside the airport terminal near the clearly marked bus stop; expect to pay up to 2,000 ptas., more in heavy traffic, plus small holiday, late-night, and/or luggage surcharges. Make sure the driver works on the meter; off-the-meter "deals" almost always cost more.

For a mere 375 ptas. there's a convenient bus to the central Plaza Colón, where a taxi can take you to your hotel. Buses leave every 15 minutes between 5:40 AM and 2 AM (slightly less often very early or late in the day). Watch your belongings, as the underground Plaza Colón bus station is a favorite haunt of purse snatchers and con artists.

The metro is a bargain at 135 ptas. per ticket (or 705 ptas. for a 10-trip ticket that can also be used on city buses), but you have to change trains to get downtown. Finally, some hotels offer shuttle service in vans; check with yours when you reserve.

Bus Travel around Madrid

Red city buses run between 6 AM and midnight and cost 130 ptas. per ride. After midnight, buses called *buyos* (night owls) run out to the suburbs from Plaza de Cibeles for the same price. There are signs at every stop listing all stops by street name, but they're hard to comprehend if you don't know the city well. Pick up a free route map from EMT kiosks on the Plaza de Cibeles or the Puerta del Sol, where you can also buy a 10-ride ticket called a Metrobus (705 ptas.) that's equally valid for the metro.

FARES & ROUTES

Pick up a free route map from EMT kiosks on the Plaza de Cibeles or the Puerta del Sol, where you can also buy a 10-ride ticket called a Metrobus (705 ptas.) that's equally valid for the metro. If you speak Spanish, call for information.

Drivers will generally make change for anything up to a 2,000-pta. note. If you've bought a 10-ride ticket, step just behind the driver and insert it in the ticket-punching machine until the mechanism goes "ding."

➤ BUS INFORMATION: **City Buses** (tel. 91/406–8810).

Bus Travel

Within Spain, an array of private companies provide service that ranges from knee-crunchingly basic to luxurious. Fares are lower than the corresponding train fares, and service is more extensive. Smaller towns don't usually have a central bus depot, so ask the tourist office where to wait for the bus to your destination. Spain's major national long-haul bus line is Enatcar. Note that service is less frequent on weekends.

For a longer haul, you can travel to Spain by bus from London or Paris. It's a long journey, but the buses are modern, and the fares are a fraction of what you'd pay to fly.

Madrid has no central bus station; buses are generally less popular than trains (though they can be faster). Most of southern Spain is served by the Estación del Sur, while buses for much of the rest of the peninsula, including Cuenca, Extremadura, Salamanca, and Valencia, depart from the Auto Res station. There are several smaller stations, however, so inquire at travel agencies for the one serving your destination.

FARES & SCHEDULES

➤ **FROM THE U.K.: Eurolines/National Express** (tel. 01582/404511 or 0990/143219).

➤ **SPANISH BUS COMPANIES: Continental Auto** (C. Alenza 20, tel. 91/533–0400; metro: Ríos Rosas), serving Cantabria and the Basque region. **Enatcar** (Calle Mendazábal, Madrid, tel. 91/527–9927). **Herranz** (departures from Fernández de los Ríos s/n, tel. 91/543–8167; metro: Moncloa), for **El Escorial and the Valle de los Caídos.** **La Sepulvedana** (Paseo de la Florida 11, near Estación de Norte, tel. 91/530–4800), serving Segovia, Ávila, and La Granja. **La Veloz** (Mediterraneo 49, tel. 91/409–7602; metro: Conde de Casal), with service to Chinchón.

➤ **BUS STATIONS: Auto Res station** (Plaza Conde de Casal 6, tel. 91/551–7200). **Estación del Sur** (Méndez Álvaro s/n, tel. 91/468–4200).

➤ **BUS TOURS: Marsans** (Gran Vía 59, Madrid,tel. 902/306090). **Pullmantur** (Plaza de Oriente 8, Madrid, tel. 91/541–1805).

Business Hours

BANKS & OFFICES

Banks are generally open weekdays from 9 to 2 and Saturday from 8:30 or 9 to 1. In summer, most banks close at 1 PM on weekdays and stay closed on Saturday. Currency exchanges at airports and train stations stay open later; you can also cash traveler's checks at El Corte Inglés department stores until 9 PM. Most government offices are open weekdays from 9 to 2 only.

MUSEUMS & SIGHTS

Most museums are open from 9:30 to 2 and 4 to 7 six days a week, usually every day but Monday. Opening hours vary, of course, and change with the high and low seasons, so confirm them before you make plans. A few large museums, such as Madrid's Prado, stay open all day.

PHARMACIES

Pharmacies keep normal business hours (9–1:30 and 5–8), but every town (or city neighborhood) has a duty pharmacy that stays open 24 hours.

SHOPS

Remember that almost all shops in Spain close at midday for at least three hours. The only exceptions are large supermarkets and the department-store chain El Corte Inglés. Stores are generally open from 9–10 to 1:30 and from 5 to 8. Most shops are closed on Sunday, and in Madrid and several other places they're also closed Saturday afternoon. That said, larger shops in tourist areas may stay open Sunday in summer and during the Christmas holiday.

Car Rental

Avis, Hertz, Budget, and National (partnered in Spain with the Spanish agency Atesa) all have branches at major Spanish airports and in large cities. Smaller, regional companies offer lower rates. All agencies have a wide range of models, but virtually all cars in Spain have a manual transmission—**if you don't want a stick shift, reserve weeks in advance and specify automatic transmission,** then call to reconfirm your automatic car before you leave for Spain. Rates in Madrid begin at the equivalents of U.S.$55 a day and $240 a week for an economy car with air-conditioning, manual transmission, and unlimited mileage. Add to this a 16% tax on car rentals.

➤ INTERNATIONAL AGENCIES: **Alamo** (tel. 800/522–9696; 020/8759–6200 in the U.K.). **Avis** (tel. 800/331–1084; 800/331–1084 in

Canada; 02/9353–9000 in Australia; 09/525–1982 in New Zealand). **Budget** (tel. 800/527–0700; 0870/607–5000 in the U.K., through affiliate Europcar). **Dollar** (tel. 800/800–6000; 0124/622–0111 in the U.K., through affiliate Sixt Kenning; 02/9223–1444 in Australia). **Hertz** (tel. 800/654–3001; 800/263–0600 in Canada; 020/8897–2072 in the U.K.; 02/9669–2444 in Australia; 09/256–8690 in New Zealand) **National Car Rental** (tel. 800/227–7368; 020/8680–4800 in the U.K., where it is known as National Europe).

➤ LOCAL AGENCIES: **National/Atesa** (tel. 902/100101).

INSURANCE

When driving a rental car, you are generally responsible for any damage to or loss of the vehicle. The collision policies sold with European rentals usually do not cover theft; before you buy insurance from the rental agency, see what coverage your personal auto-insurance policy and credit cards provide.

REQUIREMENTS & RESTRICTIONS

Your own driver's license is valid in Spain, but you may want to get an International Driver's Permit for extra assurance. Permits are available from the American or Canadian automobile association, or, in the United Kingdom, from the Automobile Association or Royal Automobile Club. Note that while anyone over 18 with a valid license can drive in Spain, some rental agencies will not rent cars to drivers under 21.

SURCHARGES

Before you pick up a car in one city and leave it in another, **ask about drop-off charges or one-way service fees,** which can be substantial. Note, too, that some rental agencies charge extra if you return the car *before* the time specified in your contract. To avoid a hefty refueling fee, **fill the tank just before you return the car,** remembering that gas stations near the rental outlet are likely to overcharge.

Children in Spain

Children are greatly indulged in Spain. You'll see kids accompanying their parents everywhere, including bars and restaurants, so bringing yours along should not be a problem. Shopkeepers will shower your child with *caramelos* (sweets), and even the coldest waiters tend to be friendlier when you have a youngster with you. And although you won't be shunted into a remote corner when you bring kids into a Spanish restaurant, you won't find high chairs or special children's menus. Children are expected to eat what their parents do, so it's perfectly acceptable to ask for an extra plate and share your food. Be prepared for late bedtimes, especially in summer—it's common to see toddlers playing cheerfully outdoors until midnight. Because children are expected to be with their parents at all times, few hotels provide baby-sitting services; but those that don't can often refer you to an independent baby-sitter (*canguro*). If you decide to rent a car, **arrange for a car seat when you reserve.**

FOOD

Visiting children may turn up their noses at some of Spain's regional specialties. Although kids seldom get their own menus, most restaurants are happy to provide simple dishes, such as plain grilled chicken, steak, or fried potatoes, for the little ones. *Pescadito frito* (batter-fried fish) is one Spanish dish that most kids do seem to enjoy. If all else fails, familiar fast-food chains such as McDonald's, Burger King, and Pizza Hut are well represented in the major cities and popular resorts.

LODGING

Most hotels in Spain allow children under a certain age to stay in their parents' room at no extra charge, but others charge them as extra adults. **Find out the cutoff age for children's discounts.**

SIGHTS & ATTRACTIONS

🐤 Sights are generally free for children up to age five. We indicate places that children might especially enjoy with a rubber duck (🐤) in the margin.

SUPPLIES & EQUIPMENT

Disposable diapers (*pañales*), formula (*papillas*), and bottled baby foods are readily available at supermarkets and pharmacies.

Customs & Duties

Keep receipts for all purchases. Upon reentering your home country, **be ready to show customs officials what you've bought.** If you feel a duty is incorrect, or you object to the way your clearance was handled, note the inspector's badge number and ask to see a supervisor. If the problem isn't resolved, write to the appropriate authorities, beginning with the port director at your point of entry.

European Union residents who have traveled only within the EU need not pass through customs upon returning to their home country. If you plan to come home with large quantities of alcohol or tobacco, check EU limits beforehand.

From countries that are not part of the European Union, visitors age 15 and over may enter Spain duty-free with up to 200 cigarettes or 50 cigars, up to one liter of alcohol over 22 proof, and up to two liters of wine. Dogs and cats are admitted as long as they have up-to-date vaccination records from their home country.

➤ INFORMATION: **Australian Customs Service** (Regional Director, Box 8, Sydney, NSW 2001, tel. 02/9213–2000, fax 02/9213–4000). **Revenue Canada** (2265 St. Laurent Blvd. S, Ottawa, Ontario K1G 4K3, tel. 613/993–0534; 800/461–9999 in Canada, fax 613/957–8911, www.ccra-adrc.gc.ca). **New Zealand Customs** (Custom House, 50 Anzac Ave., Box 29, Auckland, New Zealand, tel. 09/359–6655, fax 09/359–6732). **HM Customs and Excise** (Dorset House, Stamford St., Bromley, Kent BR1 1XX, tel. 0207/202–4227). **U.S. Customs Service** (1300 Pennsylvania Ave. NW, Washington, DC 20229, www.customs.gov; inquiries tel. 202/354–1000; complaints Office of Regulations and Rulings; registration of equipment Resource Management, tel. 202/927–0540).

Disabilities & Accessibility

Unfortunately, Spain has done little to make traveling easy for visitors with disabilities. Only the Prado and some newer museums, such as Madrid's Reina Sofía and Thyssen-Bornemisza, have wheelchair-accessible entrances or elevators. Most of the churches, castles, and monasteries on a sightseer's itinerary involve quite a bit of walking, often on uneven terrain.

RESERVATIONS
When discussing accessibility with an operator or reservations agent, **ask hard questions.** Are there any stairs, inside or out? Are there grab bars next to the toilet *and* in the shower/tub? How wide is the doorway to the room? To the bathroom? For the most extensive facilities, **opt for newer accommodations.**

TRAVEL AGENCIES
In the United States, the Americans with Disabilities Act requires that travel firms serve the needs of all travelers. Some agencies specialize in working with people with disabilities.

➤ TRAVELERS WITH MOBILITY PROBLEMS: **Access Adventures** (206 Chestnut Ridge Rd., Rochester, NY 14624, tel. 716/889–9096), run by a former physical-rehabilitation counselor. **CareVacations** (5-5110 50th Ave., Leduc, Alberta T9E 6V4, tel. 780/986–6404 or 877/478–7827, fax 780/986–8332, www.carevacations.com), for group tours and cruise vacations. **Flying Wheels Travel** (143 W. Bridge St., Box 382, Owatonna, MN 55060, tel. 507/451–5005 or 800/535–6790, fax 507/451–1685, www.flyingwheels.com).

Discounts & Deals

Be a smart shopper and **compare all your options** before making decisions. A plane ticket bought with a promotional coupon from a travel club, coupon book, or direct-mail offer may not be cheaper than the least expensive fare from a discount-ticket agency. Always keep in mind that what you get is as important as what you save.

DISCOUNT RESERVATIONS

Look into discount-reservation services, which use their buying power to get better prices on hotels, airline tickets, even car rentals. When reserving a hotel room, ask about special packages or corporate rates.

When shopping for the best deals on hotel rooms and car rentals, **look for guaranteed exchange rates,** which protect you against a falling dollar. With the rate locked in, you won't pay more even if the price goes up in the local currency.

➤ **AIRLINE TICKETS:** tel. 800/FLY–4–LESS. tel. 800/FLY–ASAP.

➤ **HOTEL ROOMS: International Marketing & Travel Concepts** (tel. 800/790–4682). **Steigenberger Reservation Service** (tel. 800/223–5652, www.srs-worldhotels.com). **Travel Interlink** (tel. 800/888–5898, www.travelinterlink.com).

PACKAGE DEALS

Don't confuse package vacations with guided tours. When you buy a package, you travel on your own, just as though you had planned the trip yourself. Fly/drive packages, which combine airfare and car rental, are often a good deal. If you **buy a rail/drive pass,** you may save on train tickets and car rentals. All Eurail- and Europass holders get a discount on Eurostar fares through the Channel Tunnel.

Driving

Driving in Madrid is best avoided by all but the bravest souls. Parking is nightmarish, traffic is extremely heavy almost all the time, and the city's daredevil drivers can be frightening. August may be an exception; the streets are then largely emptied by the mass exodus of Madrileños on vacation.

Felipe II made Madrid the capital of Spain because it was at the geographic center of his peninsular domains, and indeed many of the nation's highways radiate from Madrid like the spokes of a wheel. Originating at Kilometer 0—marked by a brass plaque on the sidewalk of the Puerta del Sol—these highways include the A6 (Segovia, Salamanca, Galicia); A1 (Burgos and the Basque Country); the N-II (Guadalajara, Barcelona, France); the N-III (Cuenca, Valencia, the Mediterranean coast); the A4 (Aranjuez, La Mancha, Granada, Seville); the N401 (Toledo); and the N-V (Talavera de la Reina, Portugal). The city is surrounded by M30 (the inner ring road) and M40 (the outer ring road), from which most of these highways are easily picked up.

Driving is the best way to see Spain's rural areas and get off the beaten track. The main cities are connected by a network of excellent four-lane *autovías* (freeways) and *autopistas* (toll freeways; "toll" is *peaje*), which are designated with the letter A and have speed limits of up to 120 km/h (74 mph). The letter N indicates a *carretera nacional* (basic national route), which may have four or two lanes. Smaller towns and villages are connected by a network of secondary roads maintained by regional, provincial, and local governments.

Spain's major routes bear heavy traffic, especially during holiday periods. Drive with care: the roads are shared by a potentially perilous mixture of local drivers, Moroccan immigrants traveling between North Africa and northern Europe, and non-Spanish vacationers, some of whom are accustomed to driving on the left side of the road. Be prepared, too, for heavy truck traffic on national routes, which, in the case of two-lane roads, can have you creeping along for hours.

AUTO CLUBS

➤ IN AUSTRALIA: **Australian Automobile Association** (tel. 02/6247–7311).

➤ IN CANADA: **Canadian Automobile Association** (CAA, tel. 613/247–0117).

➤ IN NEW ZEALAND: **New Zealand Automobile Association** (tel. 09/377–4660).

> **IN THE U.K.: Automobile Association** (AA, tel. 0990/500–600). Royal Automobile Club (RAC, tel. 0990/722–722 for membership; 0345/121–345 for insurance).

> **IN THE U.S.: American Automobile Association** (AAA, tel. 800/564–6222).

> **IN SPAIN: RACE** (José Abascal 10, Madrid, tel. 900/200093).

EMERGENCY SERVICES

The rental agencies Hertz and Avis have 24-hour breakdown service. If you belong to an auto club (AAA, CAA, or AA), you can get emergency assistance from their Spanish counterpart, RACE.

FUEL

Gas stations are plentiful, and some of those on major routes are open 24 hours. Most stations are self-service, though prices are the same as those at full-service stations. You punch in the amount of gas you want (in pesetas, not in liters), unhook the nozzle, pump the gas, and then pay. At night, however, you must pay before you fill up. Most pumps offer a choice of gas, including leaded, unleaded, and diesel, so **be careful to pick the right one** for your car. All newer cars in Spain use *gasolina sin plomo* (unleaded gas), which is available in two grades, 95 and 98 octane. *Super,* regular 97-octane leaded gas, is gradually being phased out. Although prices were decontrolled in 1993, they vary little between stations, and were at press time 148 ptas. a liter for super, 138 ptas. a liter for *sin plomo* (unleaded; 95 octane), and 152 ptas. a liter for unleaded, 98 octane. Credit cards are widely accepted.

ROAD CONDITIONS

Spain's highway system now includes some 6,000 km (3,600 mi) of beautifully maintained superhighways. Still, you'll find some stretches of major national highways that are only two lanes wide, where traffic often backs up behind slow, heavy trucks. *Autopista* tolls are steep.

Madrid has notoriously long morning and evening rush hours. If possible, **avoid the morning rush hour, which can last until noon, and the evening rush hour, which lasts from 7 to 9.**

ROAD MAPS

Detailed road maps are readily available at bookstores and gasstations.

RULES OF THE ROAD

Spaniards drive on the right. Horns are banned in cities, but that doesn't keep people from blasting away. Children under 10 may not ride in the front seat, and seat belts are compulsory everywhere. Speed limits are 50 kph (31 mph) in cities, 100 kph (62 mph) on N roads, 120 kph (74 mph) on the *autopista* or *autovía*, and, unless otherwise signposted, 90 kph (56 mph) on other roads.

Spanish highway police are particularly vigilant about speeding and illegal passing. Fines start at 15,000 ptas., and police are empowered to demand payment from non-Spanish drivers on the spot. Although local drivers, especially in cities like Madrid, will park their cars just about anywhere, you should **park only in legal spots.** Parking fines are steep, and your car might well be towed, resulting in fines, hassle, and wasted time.

Electricity

To use electric equipment from the United States, **bring a converter and adapter.** Spain's electrical current is 220 volts, 50 cycles alternating current (AC); wall outlets take Continental-type plugs, with two round prongs.

If your appliances are dual-voltage you'll need only an adapter. Don't use 110-volt outlets, marked FOR SHAVERS ONLY, for high-wattage appliances such as hair dryers. Most laptop computers operate equally well on 110 and 220 volts, so they require only an adapter.

Embassies

➤ **Embassies: Australia** (Plaza Descubridor Diegos de Ordas 3, Madrid, tel. 91/441–9300). **Canada** (Calle Nuñez de Balboa 35, Madrid, tel. 91/423–3250). **New Zealand** (Plaza Lealtad 2, Madrid, tel. 91/523–0226). **United Kingdom** (C. Fernando el Santo 16, Madrid, tel. 91/319–0200). **United States** (C. Serrano 75, Madrid, tel. 91/587–2200).

Emergencies

The pan-European emergency phone number 112 is operative in some parts of Spain, but not all. If it doesn't work, dial the emergency numbers below for national police, local police, fire department or medical services. On the road, there are emergency phones marked sos at regular intervals on *autovías* (freeways) and *autopistas* (toll highways).

➤ **Contacts Within Spain: National police** (tel. 091). **Local police** (tel. 092). **Fire department** (tel. 080).**Medical service** (tel. 061).

➤ **Hospitals in Madrid: La Paz** (Paseo de la Castellana 261, tel. 91/358–2600). **Ramon y Cajal** (Carretera de Colmenar, Km 9, tel. 91/336–8000). **12 de Octubre** (Carretera de Andalucía, Km 5.4, tel. 91/390–8000).

Etiquette & Behavior

The Spanish are very tolerant of foreigners and their strange ways, but you should always behave with courtesy. Be respectful when visiting churches: casual dress is fine if it's not gaudy or unkempt. Spaniards do object to men going bare-chested anywhere other than the beach or poolside, and generally do not look kindly on public displays of drunkenness.

When addressing Spaniards with whom you are not well acquainted, use the formal *usted* rather than the familiar *tu*. For more on language, *see* Language, *below*.

BUSINESS ETIQUETTE

Spanish office hours can be confusing to the uninitiated. Some offices stay open more or less continuously from 9 to 3, with a very short lunch break. Others open in the morning, break up the day with a long lunch break of 2–3 hours, then reopen at 4 or 5 until 7 or 8. Spaniards enjoy a certain amount of notoriety for their lack of punctuality, but this has changed dramatically in recent years: you are expected to show up for meetings on time. Smart dress is the norm. Spaniards in international fields tend to conduct business with foreigners in English. If you speak Spanish, address new colleagues with the formal usted and the corresponding verb conjugations, then follow the lead in switching to the familiar tu once a working relationship has been established.

Gay & Lesbian Travel

Since the end of Franco's dictatorship, the situation for gays and lesbians in Spain has improved dramatically: the paragraph in the Spanish civil code that made homosexuality a crime was repealed in 1978. Violence against gays does occur, but it's generally restricted to the rougher areas of very large cities.

➤ LOCAL RESOURCES: **GaiInform** (Fuencarral 37, 28004 Madrid, tel. 91/523–0070). **Teléfono Rosa** (C.Finlandia 45, Barcelona, tel. 900/601601).

Health

Sunburn and sunstroke are real risks in summertime Spain. On the hottest sunny days, even those who are not normally bothered by strong sun should cover themselves up; carry sunblock lotion; drink plenty of fluids; and limit sun time for the first few days.

If you require medical attention, ask your hotel's front desk for assistance or go to the nearest public Centro de Salud (day hospital); in serious cases, you'll be referred to the regional hospital. Medical care is good in Spain, but nursing is perfunctory, as relatives are expected to stop by and look after inpatients' needs. In some popular destinations, such as the Costa del Sol, there are volunteer English interpreters on hand.

Spain was recently documented as having the highest number of AIDS cases in Europe. Those applying for work permits will be asked for proof of HIV-negative status.

OVER-THE-COUNTER REMEDIES

Over-the-counter remedies are available at any *farmacia* (pharmacy). Some will look familiar, such as *aspirina* (aspirin), while other medications are sold under various brand names. If you regularly take a non-prescription medicine, take a sample box or bottle with you, and the Spanish pharmacist will provide you with its local equivalent.

Holidays

In 2001, Spain's national holidays include: January 1, January 6 (Epiphany), April 13 (Good Friday), May 1 (May Day), August 15 (Assumption), October 12 (National Day), November 1 (All Saints), December 6 (Constitution), December 8 (Immaculate Conception), and December 25.

In addition, each region, city, and town has its own holidays honoring political events and patron saints. Madrid holidays include May 2 (Madrid Day), May 15 (St. Isidro), and November 9 (Almudena).

If a public holiday falls on a Tuesday or Thursday, remember that many businesses also close on the nearest Monday or Friday for a long weekend called a *puente* (bridge). If a major holiday falls on a Sunday, businesses close on Monday.

Insurance

The most useful travel-insurance plan is a comprehensive policy that includes coverage for trip cancellation and interruption, default, trip delay, and medical expenses (with a waiver for preexisting conditions).

Without insurance you will lose all or most of your money if you cancel your trip, regardless of the reason. Default insurance covers you if your tour operator, airline, or cruise line goes out of business. Trip-delay covers expenses that arise because of bad weather or mechanical delays. Study the fine print when comparing policies.

On international trips, a key component of travel insurance is coverage for medical bills incurred if you get sick on the road. Such expenses are not generally covered by Medicare or private policies. U.K. residents can buy a travel-insurance policy valid for most vacations taken that year, but check the rules concerning preexisting conditions. British and Australian citizens need extra medical coverage when traveling overseas.

Always **buy a travel policy directly from the insurance company.** If you buy it from a cruise line, airline, or tour operator that goes out of business, you will probably not be covered for the agency or operator's default, a major risk. Before making any purchase, **review your existing health and homeowner's policies** to find what they cover away from home.

➤ TRAVEL INSURERS: In the U.S.: **Access America** (6600 W. Broad St., Richmond, VA 23230, tel. 804/285–3300 or 800/284–8300, fax 804/673–1583, www.previewtravel.com), **Travel Guard International** (1145 Clark St., Stevens Point, WI 54481, tel. 715/345–0505 or 800/826–1300, fax 800/955–8785, www.noelgroup.com). **In Canada: Voyager Insurance** (44 Peel Center Dr., Brampton, Ontario L6T 4M8, tel. 905/791–8700; 800/668–4342 in Canada).

➤ INSURANCE INFORMATION: In the U.K.: **Association of British Insurers** (51–55 Gresham St., London EC2V 7HQ, tel. 0207/600–3333, fax 0207/696–8999, www.abi.org.uk). **In Australia: Insurance Council of Australia** (tel. 03/9614–1077, fax 03/9614–7924).

Language

Spanish is referred to as Castellano, or Castilian, and your efforts to speak it will be graciously received. Learn at least the following basic phrases: *buenos días* (hello—until 2 PM), *buenas tardes* (good afternoon—until 8 PM), *buenas noches* (hello—after dark), *por favor* (please), *gracias* (thank you), *adiós* (good-bye), *sí* (yes), *no* (no), *los servicios* (the toilets), *la cuenta* (bill/check), *habla inglés?* (do you speak English?), *no comprendo* (I don't understand). For more helpful expressions, *see* the Spanish Vocabulary following Smart Travel Tips, or, better yet, pick up a copy of *Fodor's Spanish for Travelers*.

If your Spanish breaks down, you should have no trouble finding people who speak English in Madrid, but you won't necessarily be able to count on the bus driver or the passerby on the street. Those who do speak English may speak the British variety, so don't be surprised if you're told to queue (line up) or take the lift (elevator) to the loo (toilet). Many guided tours offered at museums and historic sites are in Spanish; ask about the language that will be spoken before you sign up.

▶ PHRASE BOOK & LANGUAGE TAPES: *Fodor's Spanish for Travelers* (tel. 800/733–3000 in the U.S.; 800/668–4247 in Canada; $7 for phrasebook, $16.95 for audio set).

Lodging

The lodgings we review are the cream of the crop in each price category. We always list the facilities available, but we don't specify whether they cost extra; so when pricing accommodations, always ask what's included and what's not.

APARTMENT & VILLA RENTALS

If you want a home base that's roomy enough for a family and comes with cooking facilities, **consider a furnished rental.** These can save you money, especially if you're traveling with a group. Home-exchange directories sometimes list rentals as well as exchanges.

➤ INTERNATIONAL AGENTS: **Hideaways International** (767 Islington St., Portsmouth, NH 03801, tel. 603/430–4433 or 800/843–4433, fax 603/430–4444, www.hideaways.com; membership $99). **Hometours International** (Box 11503, Knoxville, TN 37939, tel. 865/690–8484 or 800/367–4668). **Interhome** (1990 N.E. 163rd St., Suite 110, N. Miami Beach, FL 33162, tel. 305/940–2299 or 800/882–6864, fax 305/940–2911, www.interhome.com). **Vacation Home Rentals Worldwide** (235 Kensington Ave., Norwood, NJ 07648, tel. 201/767–9393 or 800/633–3284, fax 201/767–5510). **Villas and Apartments Abroad** (1270 Avenue of the Americas, 15th floor, New York, NY 10020, tel. 212/897–5045 or 800/433–3020, fax 212/897–5039, www.vaanyc.com). **Villas International** (950 Northgate Dr., Suite 206, San Rafael, CA 94903, tel. 415/499–9490 or 800/221–2260, fax 415/499–9491, www.villasintl.com).

HOME EXCHANGES

If you'd like to exchange your home for someone else's temporarily, **join a home-exchange organization,** which will send you its updated listings of available exchanges for a year and include your own listing in at least one of them. You make the arrangements yourself.

➤ EXCHANGE CLUBS: **HomeLinkInternational** (Box 650, Key West, FL 33041, tel. 305/294–7766 or 800/638–3841, fax 305/294–1448, www.homelink.org; $98 per year). **Intervac U.S.** (Box 590504, San Francisco, CA 94159, tel. 800/756–4663, fax 415/435–7440, www.intervac.com; $89 per year includes two catalogues).

HOSTELS

No matter what your age, you can **cut lodging costs by staying in hostels.** In some 5,000 locations in more than 70 countries around the world, Hostelling International (HI), the umbrella group for a number of national youth-hostel associations, offers single-sex, dorm-style beds and, in many hostels, rooms for couples and family accommodations. Membership in any HI national hostel association, open to travelers of all ages, allows you to stay in HI-affiliated hostels at member rates; one-year membership is about U.S.$25 for adults (C$26.75 in Canada, £9.30 in the U.K., $30 in Australia, and $30 in New Zealand). Members have priority if the hostel is full; they're also eligible for discounts around the world, even on rail and bus travel in some countries.

➤ ORGANIZATIONS: **Hostelling International—American Youth Hostels** (733 15th St. NW, Suite 840, Washington, DC 20005, tel. 202/783–6161, fax 202/783–6171, www.hiayh.org). **Hostelling International—Canada** (400–205 Catherine St., Ottawa, Ontario K2P 1C3, tel. 613/237–7884, fax 613/237–7868, www.hostellingintl.ca). **Youth Hostel Association of England and Wales** (Trevelyan House, 8 St. Stephen's Hill, St. Albans, Hertfordshire AL1 2DY, tel. 01727/855215 or 01727/845047, fax 01727/844126, www.yha.uk). **Australian Youth Hostel Association** (10 Mallett St., Camperdown, NSW 2050, tel. 02/9565–1699, fax 02/9565–1325, www.yha.com.au). **Youth Hostels Association of New Zealand** (Box 436, Christchurch, New Zealand, tel. 03/379–9970, fax 03/365–4476, www.yha.org.nz).

HOTELS

➤ MAJOR SPANISH HOTEL CHAINS: **Hotusa** (tel. 93/319–9062). **NH Hoteles** (tel. 902/115116, www.nh-hoteles.es). **Sol Meliá** (tel. 902/144444, www.solmelia.es). **Tryp** (tel. 901/116199).

Mail & Shipping

Spain's postal system, the *correos*, does work, but delivery times can vary widely. An airmail letter to the United States may take anywhere from four days to two weeks; delivery to other destinations is equally unpredictable. Sending your letters by priority mail ("*urgente*") ensures speedier arrival.

OVERNIGHT SERVICES

When time is of the essence, or when you're sending valuable items or documents overseas, you can use a courier (*mensajero*). The major international agencies, such as Federal Express and UPS, have representatives in Spain; the biggest Spanish courier service is Seur.

➤ MAJOR SERVICES: **DHL** (tel. 902/122424). **Federal Express** (tel. 900/100871). **MRW** (tel. 900/300400). **Seur** (tel. 902/101010). **UPS** (tel. 900/102410).

POSTAL RATES

Airmail letters to the United States and Canada cost 115 ptas. up to 20 grams. Letters to the United Kingdom and other EU countries cost 70 ptas. up to 20 grams. Letters within Spain are 35 ptas. Postcards are charged the same rates as letters. You can buy stamps at post offices and at licensed tobacco shops.

RECEIVING MAIL

Because mail delivery in Spain can often be slow and unreliable, it's best to have your mail sent to American Express. Mail can also be held at a Spanish post office; have it addressed to Lista de Correos (the equivalent of Poste Restante) in a town you'll be visiting. Postal addresses should include the name of the province in parentheses.

➤ INFORMATION: In the U.S., call **American Express** (tel. 800/528–4800) for a list of offices overseas.

Metro Travel

Madrid's metro is quick, frequent, and, at 135 ptas. no matter how far you travel, cheap. Even cheaper is the 10-ride Metrobus ticket, or *billete de diez*, which costs 705 ptas., is also valid for buses, and is accepted by automatic turnstiles (lines at ticket booths can be long). The system is open from 6 AM to 1:30 AM, though a few entrances close earlier. There are 10 metro lines, and system maps in every station detail their color-coded routes. Note the end station of the line you need, and just follow signs to the correct corridor. Exits are marked SALIDA.

Money

Spain is no longer a budget destination, but prices still compare slightly favorably to those elsewhere in Europe. Coffee in a bar generally costs 125 ptas. (standing) or 150 ptas. (seated). Beer in a bar: 125 ptas. standing, 150 ptas. seated. Small glass of wine in a bar: 100 ptas. Soft drink: 150–200 ptas. a bottle. Ham-and-cheese sandwich: 300–450 ptas. Two-kilometer (1-mile) taxi ride: 400 ptas., but the meter keeps ticking in traffic jams. Local bus or subway ride: 135–150 ptas. Movie ticket: 500–800 ptas. Foreign newspaper: 300 ptas. In this book we quote prices for adults only, but note that children, students, and senior citizens almost always pay substantially reduced fees. For information on taxes in Spain, *see* Taxes, *below.*

CREDIT CARDS

Throughout this book, the following abbreviations are used: **AE,** American Express; **DC,** Diner's Club; **MC,** MasterCard; and **V,** Visa.

➤ REPORTING LOST CARDS: **American Express** (tel. 900/941413). **Diners Club** (tel. 901/101011). **MasterCard** (tel. 900/974445). **Visa** (tel. 900/971231).

CURRENCY

As of January 1, 1999, Spain's official currency is the European monetary unit, the Euro. Prices are often quoted in both pesetas and Euros—convenient for Americans, as the Euro is close in value to a U.S. dollar—but until 2002 the Euro will be used only on the level of trade and banking, so the peseta (pta.) continues to be legal tender. You can, however, purchase traveler's checks in Euros, convenient if you'll be traveling to more than one Euro-denominated country (Austria, Belgium, Finland, France, Germany, Ireland, Italy, Luxembourg, the Netherlands, Portugal, and Spain). Spanish bills are worth 10,000, 5,000, 2,000, and

1,000 ptas.; coins are 500, 200, 100, 50, 25, 10, 5, and 1 pta. Be careful not to confuse the 100- and 500-pta. coins—they're the same color and almost the same size. Five-pta. coins are called *duros*. At press time exchange rates were extremely favorable for English-speaking travelers: 184 ptas. to the U.S. dollar, 124 ptas. to the Canadian dollar, 276 ptas. to the pound sterling, 160 ptas. to the Australian dollar, and 88 ptas. to the New Zealand dollar. One Euro was worth U.S. 90¢.

CURRENCY EXCHANGE

For the most favorable exchange rates, **change money in banks.** Although ATM transaction fees may be higher abroad than at home, ATM rates are excellent because they're based on wholesale rates offered only by major banks. You won't do as well at exchange booths in airports or train and bus stations, in hotels, in restaurants, or in stores. To avoid standing in line at an airport exchange booth, **get a bit of Spanish currency before you leave home.**

➤ EXCHANGE SERVICES: **International Currency Express** (tel. 888/278–6628 for orders, www.foreignmoney.com). **Thomas Cook Currency Services** (tel. 800/287–7362 for phone orders and retail locations, www.us.thomascook.com).

TRAVELER'S CHECKS

Traveler's checks are widely accepted in cities. If you'll be staying in small towns or rural areas, bring extra cash. Lost or stolen checks can usually be replaced within 24 hours. To ensure a speedy refund, buy your own traveler's checks—don't let someone else pay for them—and make the call yourself if you need to request a refund. Irregularities can cause delays.

Packing

Pack light. Although baggage carts are free and plentiful in most Spanish airports, they're rare in train and bus stations.

On the whole, Spaniards dress up more than Americans or the British. It makes sense to wear casual, comfortable clothing and shoes for sightseeing, but you'll want to **dress up a bit, especially for fine restaurants and nightclubs.** American tourists are easily spotted for their sneakers—to blend in, wear leather shoes.

In your carry-on luggage, **pack an extra pair of eyeglasses or contact lenses and enough of any medication you take** to last the entire trip. You can also ask your doctor to write a spare prescription using the drug's generic name, since brand names may vary from country to country. **Never pack prescription drugs or valuables** in luggage to be checked. To avoid delays in customs, carry medications in their original packaging. Finally, don't forget to **carry the addresses of offices that handle refunds of lost traveler's checks.**

CHECKING LUGGAGE

Your airline decides how many bags (or how much weight) you can carry onto the plane. Most, but not all, allow two bags, so make sure that everything you carry aboard will fit under your seat or in the overhead bin, and line up for boarding early for the best dibs on bin space. Note that if you have a seat at the back of the plane, you'll probably board first, while the overhead bins are still empty.

Label each of your bags with your name, address, and phone number (if you use your home address, cover it so potential thieves can't see it readily). **Pack a copy of your itinerary** inside each piece of luggage. When you check in, **make sure that each bag is correctly tagged** with the destination airport's three-letter code. If your bags arrive damaged or fail to arrive at all, file a written report with the airline *before* leaving the airport.

Passports & Visas

Make two photocopies of your passport's data page—one for someone at home and another for you, carried separately from your passport. If you lose your passport, promptly call the nearest embassy or consulate *and* the local police.

ENTERING SPAIN

Visitors from the U.S., Australia, Canada, New Zealand, and the U.K. need a valid passport to enter Spain. Australians who wish to stay longer than a month also need a visa, available from the Spanish Embassy in Canberra.

PASSPORT OFFICES

The best time to apply for a passport, or to renew your old one, is in fall or winter. Before any trip, check your passport's expiration date, and, if necessary, renew it as soon as possible.

➤ AUSTRALIAN CITIZENS: **Passport Office** (tel. 131–232, www.dfat.gov.au/passports).

➤ CANADIAN CITIZENS: **Passport Office Information Service** (tel. 819/994–3500 or 800/567–6868, www.dfait-maeci.gc.ca/passport).

➤ NEW ZEALAND CITIZENS: **Passport Office** (tel. 04/494–0700, www.passports.govt.nz).

➤ U.K. CITIZENS: **Passport Agency** (tel. 0990/210410, www.ukpa.gov.uk/ukpass.htm).

➤ U.S. CITIZENS: **National Passport Information Center** (tel. 900/ 225–5674; 35¢ per minute for automated service, $1.05 per minute for operator service; http://travel.state.gov/passport _services.html).

Rest Rooms

Spain has some public rest rooms, including, in larger cities like Madrid, small coin-operated booths. Your best option, however, is to use the facilities in a bar or cafeteria, remembering that it's customary to order a drink in such cases. Gas stations have rest rooms, but you usually have to request the key to use them.

Safety

Petty crime is a major problem in Madrid and elsewhere in Spain. The most frequent offenses are pickpocketing, mugging, and theft from cars. We cannot overemphasize the fact that you should **never, ever leave anything valuable in a parked car,** no matter how friendly the area feels, how quickly you'll return, or how invisible the item seems once you lock it in the trunk. Thieves can spot rental cars a mile away, and they work very efficiently. In airports, laptop computers are choice prey.

WOMEN IN MADRID

The traditional Spanish custom of the *piropo* (a shouted "compliment" to women walking down the street) is fast disappearing, though women traveling alone may still encounter it on occasion. The piropo is harmless, if annoying, and should simply be ignored.

Sightseeing Tours

Contact the Asociación Profesional de Informadores to hire a personal guide. Your hotel can arrange standard city tours in either English or Spanish; most offer Madrid Artístico (including the Royal Palace and the Prado), Madrid Panorámico (a half-day tour for first-time visitors), Madrid de Noche (combinations include a flamenco or a nightclub show), and Panorámico y Toros (on Sunday, a brief city overview followed by a bullfight). The Municipal Tourist Office arranges tours of Madrid's old quarters in English every Saturday morning, departing from the tourist office on the Plaza Mayor at 10.

The *ayuntamiento* (city hall) has a popular selection of Spanish bus and walking tours under the rubric "Descubre Madrid." The walking tours, which depart most mornings, visit many hidden corners as well as major sights; options include "Madrid's Railroads," "Medicine in Madrid," "Goya's Madrid," and "Commerce and Finance in Madrid." Schedules are listed in the leaflet available from the municipal tourist office. Buy tickets at the Patronato de Turismo. For day trips to sights outside Madrid, such as El Escorial, contact Juliá Tours.

Trapsatur runs the Madrid Visión tourist bus, which makes a 1½-hour sightseeing circuit of the city with recorded commentary in English. No advance reservation is needed; just show up at Gran Vía 32. Buses also leave from the front of the Prado Museum every 1½ hours beginning at 12:30 Monday–Saturday, 10:30 on Sunday. A round-trip ticket costs 1,500 ptas.; a day pass, which allows you to get on and off at various attractions, is 2,000 ptas. An identical hop-on, hop-off service on an open-top double decker is operated by Sol Pentours, whose daily tours leave every half hour from Plaza de España, in front of the Crowne Plaza Hotel, between 10 AM and 8 PM. The fare is 1,600 ptas., and the complete ride takes 90 minutes.

➤ INFORMATION: **Asociación Profesional de Informadores** (Ferraz 82, tel. 91/542–1214 or 91/541–1221). **Municipal Tourist Office** (Plaza Mayor 3, tel. 91/588–2900). **Julià Tours** (Gran Ví 68, tel. 91/559–9605). **Patronato de Turismo** (C. Mayor 69, tel. 91/588–2900). **Sol Pentours** (Gran Vía 26, tel. 902/303903). **Trapsatur** (tel. 91/302–6039).

Taxes

VALUE-ADDED TAX

Value-added tax, similar to sales tax, is called IVA in Spain (pronounced "ee-vah"; for impuesto sobre el valor añadido). It is levied on both products and services such as hotel rooms and restaurant meals. When in doubt about whether tax is included, ask, "Está incluido el IVA"?

The IVA rate for hotels and restaurants is 7%, regardless of their number of stars or forks. Menus will generally say at the bottom whether tax is included (IVA incluido) or not (más 7% IVA).

While food, pharmaceuticals, and household items are taxed at the lowest rate, most consumer goods are taxed at 16%. A number of shops, particularly large stores and boutiques in holiday resorts, participate in Global Refund (formerly Europe Tax-Free Shopping), a V.A.T. refund service that makes getting your money back relatively hassle-free. On purchases of more than 15,000 ptas., you're entitled to a refund of the 16% tax. **Ask for the Global Refund form** (called a Shopping Cheque) in participating stores. You show your passport and fill out the form; the vendor then mails you the refund, or—often more convenient—you **present your original receipt to the VAT office at the airport** when you leave Spain. (In both Madrid, the office is near the duty-free shops. Save time for this process, as lines can be long.) Customs signs the original and refunds your money on the spot in cash (pesetas), or sends it to their central office to process a credit-card refund. Credit-card refunds take a few weeks.

Taxis

Taxis are one of Madrid's few truly good deals. Meters start at 190 ptas. and add 95 ptas. per km (⅝ mi) thereafter (125 ptas. per km at night, on weekends and holidays, and beyond city limits). Numerous supplemental charges, however, mean that your total cost often bears little resemblance to what you see on the meter. Supplemental charges—over and above your fare—include 150 ptas. on Sundays and holidays and between 11 PM and 6 AM, 150 ptas. to sports stadiums or the bullring, and 400 ptas. (plus 50 ptas. per suitcase) to or from the airport.

Stands are numerous, and taxis are easily hailed in the street—except when it rains, at which point they're exceedingly hard to come by. Available cabs display a LIBRE sign during the day, a green light at night. You can also call one of Madrid's radio-taxi companies to send a car your way.

➤ RADIO-TAXI COMPANIES: Radio Taxi Gremial (tel. 91/447–5180). Radioteléfono Taxi (tel. 91/547–8200). Tele-Taxi (tel. 91/371–2131).

Telephones

Spain's phone system, Telefónica, is perfectly efficient. Direct dialing is the norm. Note that only cell phones conforming to the European GSM standard will work in Spain.

AREA & COUNTRY CODES

The country code for Spain is 34, and the area code for Madrid is 91. Phoning home: country codes are 1 for the United States and Canada, 44 for the United Kingdom, 61 for Australia, and 64 for New Zealand.

DIRECTORY & OPERATOR ASSISTANCE

For general information in Spain, dial 1003. International operators, who generally speak English, are at 025.

INTERNATIONAL CALLS

International calls are awkward from coin-operated pay phones because of the enormous number of coins needed; and they can be expensive from hotels, as the hotel often adds a hefty surcharge. The best way to phone home is to use a public phone that accepts phone cards (☞ Phone Cards, *below*) or go to the local telephone office, the *locutorio*. (Madrid's main one is at Gran Vía 28. There's another at the main post office, and a third at Paseo Recoletos 43, just off Plaza Colón.) You converse in a quiet, private booth, and you're charged according to the meter. If the call ends up costing 500 ptas. or more, you can pay with Visa or MasterCard. To make an international call yourself, dial 00, then the country code, then the area code and number.

LOCAL CALLS

All area codes begin with a 9. To call within Spain—even locally—dial the area code first. Numbers preceded by a 900 code are toll-free; those starting with a 6 are going to a cellular phone. Note that calls to cell phones are significantly more expensive than calls to regular phones.

LONG-DISTANCE SERVICES

AT&T, MCI, and Sprint access codes make calling long distance relatively convenient, but you may find the local access number blocked in many hotel rooms. First ask the hotel operator to connect you. If the hotel operator can't comply, ask for an international operator, or dial the international operator yourself. One way to improve your odds of getting connected to your long-distance carrier is to travel with more than one company's calling card (a hotel may block Sprint, for example, but not MCI). If all else fails, call from a pay phone.

➤ **ACCESS CODES: AT&T USADirect** (tel. 800/222–0300). MCI WorldCom (tel. 800/444–4444). Sprint Express (tel. 800/793–1153).

➤ **ACCESS CODES IN SPAIN: AT&T** (tel. 900/990011). **MCI** (tel. 900/990014). **Sprint** (tel. 900/990013).

PHONE CARDS

To use a newer pay phone you need a special phone card (*tarjeta telefónica*), which you can buy at any tobacco shop or newsstand, in denominations of 1,000 or 2,000 ptas. Some such phones also accept credit cards, but phone cards are more reliable.

PUBLIC PHONES

You'll find pay phones in individual booths, in locutorios, and in many bars and restaurants. Most have a digital readout so you can see your money ticking away. If you're calling with coins, you need at least 25 ptas. to call locally, 75 ptas. to call another province. Simply insert the coins and wait for a dial tone. (With older models, you line coins up in a groove on top of the dial and they drop down as needed.)

Time

Spain is on Central European Time, one hour ahead of Greenwich Mean Time, six hours ahead of Eastern Standard Time. Like the rest of the European Union, Spain switches to daylight saving time on the last weekend in March, and switches back on the last weekend in October.

Tipping

Waiters and other service staff expect to be tipped, and you can be sure that your contribution will be appreciated. On the other hand, if you experience bad or surly service, don't feel obligated to leave a tip.

Restaurant checks almost always include service, which is not the same as a voluntary tip. **Do not tip more than 10% of the bill,** and leave less if you eat tapas or sandwiches at a bar—just enough to round out the bill to the nearest 100. Tip cocktail servers 50–75 ptas. a drink, depending on the bar.

Tip taxi drivers about 10% of the total fare; add more for long rides or extra help with luggage. Note that rides from airports carry an official surcharge plus a small handling fee for each piece of luggage. Tip hotel porters 100 ptas. a bag, the bearer of room service 100 ptas, concierges according to service, tour guides 300 ptas., theater or bullfight ushers 25–50 ptas., barbers 100 ptas., women's hairdressers 200 ptas., and restroom attendants 25 ptas.

Tour Operators

Because everything is prearranged on a guided tour, you'll spend less time planning—and often get it all for a reasonable price.

BOOKING WITH AN AGENT

Travel agents are excellent resources. Do collect brochures from several agencies, however, as some agents' suggestions may be influenced by relationships with tour and package firms that reward them for volume sales. If you have a special interest, **find an agent with expertise in that area**; ASTA (☞ Travel Agencies, *below*) has a database of specialists worldwide.

Make sure your travel agent is familiar with the rooms and other services in any hotel he or she recommends. Ask about the hotel's location, room size, beds, and whether the hotel has any specific amenities you need. Has your agent been there in person or sent others whom you can contact?

Do some homework: local tourism boards can provide information about lesser-known and small-niche operators, some of which may sell only directly.

BUYER BEWARE

Every year consumers are stranded or lose their money when tour operators—even large ones with excellent reputations—go out of business. **Check out the operator.** Ask several travel agents about its reputation, and try to **go with a company that has a consumer-protection program.** (Look for information in the company's brochure.) In the United States, members of the National Tour Association and the United States Tour Operators Association are required to set aside funds to cover your payments and travel arrangements in the event that the company defaults. It's also a good idea to choose a company that participates in the American Society of Travel Agents' Tour Operator Program (TOP); ASTA will act as mediator in any disputes between you and your tour operator.

Remember that the more your package or tour includes, the better you can predict the ultimate cost of your vacation. Make sure you know exactly what is covered, and **beware of hidden costs.** Are taxes, tips, and transfers included? Entertainment and excursions? These can add up.

➤ TOUR-OPERATOR RECOMMENDATIONS: **American Society of Travel Agents** (☞ Travel Agencies, *below*). **National Tour Association** (NTA; 546 E. Main St., Lexington, KY 40508, tel. 606/226–4444 or 800/682–8886, www.ntaonline.com). **United States Tour Operators Association** (USTOA; 342 Madison Ave., Suite 1522, New York, NY 10173, tel. 212/599–6599 or 800/468–7862, fax 212/599–6744, www.ustoa.com).

Train Travel

For routes with convenient schedules, trains are the most economical way to go. First- and second-class seats are reasonably priced, and you can get a bunk in a compartment with five other people for a supplement of about U.S.$25.

International overnight trains run from Madrid to Lisbon. A daytime train runs from Barcelona to Grenoble and Geneva (10 hours). If you purchase a same-day round-trip ticket while in Spain, you'll get a 20% discount; if you purchase a different-day round-trip ticket, a 10% discount applies.

Spain's wonderful high-speed train, the 180-mph AVE, travels between Madrid and Seville (with a stop in Córdoba) in less than three hours at prices starting around 10,000 ptas. each way. The fast Talgo service is also efficient. However, the rest of the state-run rail system—known as RENFE—remains below par by European standards. Local train travel can be tediously slow, and most long-distance trips run at night. While overnight trains have comfortable sleeper cars, first-class fares that include a sleeping compartment are comparable to airfares. Commuter trains and most long-distance trains forbid smoking, though some long-distance trains have smoking cars.

Most Spaniards buy train tickets in advance by standing in long lines at the station. The overworked clerks rarely speak English, however, so if you don't speak Spanish, you're better off going to a travel agency that displays the blue-and-yellow RENFE sign. The price is the same. You can also reserve by phone, charge your tickets to a credit card, and have them delivered to your hotel. Note that if your itinerary is set in stone and has little room for error, you can buy RENFE tickets through Rail Europe (☞ *below*) before you leave home.

Madrid has three main train stations: *estaciones* Chamartín, Atocha, and Norte. Remember to confirm which station you need when arranging a trip. Generally speaking, Chamartín, near the northern tip of Paseo Castellana, serves trains bound for points north and west, including Barcelona, San Sebastián, Burgos, León, Oviedo, La Coruña, and Salamanca, as well as France and Portugal. Atocha, at the southern end of Paseo del Prado, provides AVE (high-speed) train service to Córdoba and Seville and regular service to points mainly south and east, including El Escorial, Segovia, Toledo, Seville, Málaga, Córdoba,

Valencia, and Castellón. Norte is primarily for local trains serving Madrid's western suburbs.

CUTTING COSTS

If you're coming from the United States or Canada and planning extensive train travel, **look into rail passes.** If Spain is your only destination, consider a Spain Flexipass. Prices begin at U.S.$150 for three days of second-class travel within a two-month period and $190 for first class. Other passes cover more days and longer periods.

Spain is one of 17 European countries in which you can use the Eurailpass, which buys you unlimited first-class rail travel in all participating countries for the duration of the pass. If you plan to rack up the miles, get a standard pass. These are available for 15 days ($544), 21 days ($718), one month ($890), two months ($1,260), and three months ($1,558). If your needs are more limited, look into a Europass, which costs less than a Eurailpass and buys you a limited number of travel days, in a limited number of countries (France, Germany, Italy, Spain, and Switzerland), during a specified time period.

In addition to the Eurailpass and Europass, Rail Europe sells the Eurail Youthpass (for those under age 26), the Eurail Saverpass (which gives a discount for two or more people traveling together), a Eurail Flexipass (which allows a certain number of travel days within a set period), the Euraildrive Pass, and the Europass Drive (which combines travel by train and rental car). Whichever you choose, remember that you must **buy your pass before you leave** for Europe.

Many travelers assume that rail passes guarantee them seats on the trains they wish to ride: not so. You need to **reserve seats in advance** even if you're using a rail pass. Seat reservations are required on some trains, particularly high-speed trains, and are wise on any train that might be crowded. You'll also need a reservation if you want a sleeping berth.

➤ GENERAL INFORMATION: **Atocha** (tel. 91/328–9020). **Chamartín** (tel. 91/315–9976). **RENFE** (tel. 902/240202, www.renfe.es).

➤ RAIL PASSES: **Rail Europe** (226–230 Westchester Ave., White Plains, NY 10604, tel. 914/682–5172 or 800/438–7245;2087 Dundas E, Suite 105, Mississauga, Ontario, Canada L4X1M2, tel. 416/602–4195; www.raileurope.com). **DER Tours** (Box 1606, Des Plaines, IL 60017, tel. 800/782–2424, fax 800/282–7474). **CIT Tours Corp.** (342 Madison Ave., Suite 207, New York, NY 10173, tel. 212/697–2100; 800/248–8687; 800/248–7245 in western U.S.).

FROM THE U.K.
Train services to Spain from the United Kingdom are not as frequent, fast, or affordable as flights, and you have to change trains (and stations) in Paris. Allow two hours for the changing process, then 13 hours for the trip from Paris to Madrid. It's worth paying extra for a Talgo express or the Puerta del Sol express to avoid having to change trains again at the Spanish border. If you're under 26 years old, Eurotrain has excellent deals.

➤ INFORMATION: **British Rail Travel Centers** (tel. 0207/834–2345). Eurotrain (52 Grosvenor Gardens, London SW1W OAG, U.K., tel. 0207/730–3402). **Transalpino** (71–75 Buckingham Palace Rd., London SW1W ORE, U.K., tel. 0207/834–9656).

Travel Agencies

A good travel agent puts your needs first. Look for an agency that has been in business at least five years, emphasizes customer service, and has someone on staff who specializes in your destination. In addition, **make sure the agency belongs to a professional trade organization.** The American Society of Travel Agents (ASTA), with 27,000 agents in some 170 countries, is the largest and most influential in the field. Operating under the motto "Integrity in Travel," it maintains and enforces a strict code of ethics and will step in to help mediate any agent-client disputes if necessary. ASTA also maintains a Web site that includes a directory of member agents. (If a travel agency is also acting as your tour operator, *see* Buyer Beware *in* Tours & Packages, *above*.)

➤ **AGENTS IN MADRID: American Express** (Next to Cortés (parliament building) on Génova, Plaza de las Cortés 2, tel. 91/322–5500). **Carlson Wagons-Lits** (Paseo de la Castellana 96, tel. 91/563–1202). **Madrid & Beyond** (Gran Vía 59-8D, tel. 91/758–0063, fax 91/542–4391). **Pullmantur** (Across from Royal Palace, Plaza de Oriente 8, tel. 91/541–1807).

➤ **AGENT REFERRALS: American Society of Travel Agents** (ASTA; tel. 800/965–2782 24-hr hot line, fax 703/684–8319, www.astanet.com). **Association of British Travel Agents** (68–71 Newman St., London W1P 4AH, tel. 0207/637–2444, fax 0207/637–0713, www.abtanet.com). **Association of Canadian Travel Agents** (1729 Bank St., Suite 201, Ottawa, Ontario K1V 7Z5, tel. 613/521–0474, fax 613/521–0805). **Australian Federation of Travel Agents** (Level 3, 309 Pitt St., Sydney 2000, tel. 02/9264–3299, fax 02/9264–1085, www.afta.com.au). **Travel Agents' Association of New Zealand** (Box 1888, Wellington 10033, tel. 04/499–0104, fax 04/499–0827).

Visitor Information

Madrid has four regional tourist offices. The best is on Duque de Medinaceli 2, near the Palace Hotel, open weekdays 9–7 and Saturday 9–1. The others are at Barajas Airport; the Chamartín train station, open weekdays 8–8 and Saturday 9–1; and the remote Mercado de la Puerta de Toledo, open weekdays 9–7 and Saturday 9–1. The Municipal Tourist Office on the Plaza Mayor is the place to arrange English-language tours of Madrid's old quarters; it's open weekdays 10–8, Saturday 10–2, and Sunday 10–2.

➤ **TOURIST OFFICE OF SPAIN: Chicago** (845 N. Michigan Ave., Chicago, IL 60611, tel. 312/642–1992, fax 312/642–9817). **Los Angeles** (8383

Wilshire Blvd., Suite 960, Beverly Hills, CA 90211, tel. 213/658–7188, fax 213/658–1061). **Miami** (1221 Brickell Ave., Suite 1850, Miami, FL 33131, tel. 305/358–1992, fax 305/358–8223). **New York** (666 5th Ave., 35th floor, New York, NY 10103, tel. 212/265–8822, fax 212/265–8864). **Canada** (2 Bloor St. W, 34th floor, Toronto, Ontario M4W 3E2, Canada, tel. 416/961–3131, fax 416/961–1992). **United Kingdom** (22–23 Manchester Sq., London W1M 5AP, U.K., tel. 0207/486–8977, fax 0207/486–8034).

➤ Tourist Offices in Madrid: **Barajas Airport Office** (tel. 91/305–8656). **Chamartín Office** (tel. 91/315–9976). **Duque de Medinaceli 2 Office** (tel. 91/429–4951). **Mercado de la Puerta de Toledo Office** (Glorieta Puerta de Toledo, 3rd floor, tel. 91/364–1876). **Municipal Tourist Office** (tel. 91/366–5477).

Web Sites

Check out the World Wide Web when you're planning. You'll find everything from up-to-date weather forecasts to virtual tours of major cities. Fodor's own Web site, www.fodors.com, is a great place to start your on-line travels. For more information on Spain, visit www.okspain.org, www.tourspain.es, www.cyberspain.com, and www.red2000.com/spain.

When to Go

May and October are the optimal times to come to Spain, as the weather is generally warm and dry. May gives you more hours of daylight, while October offers a chance to enjoy the harvest season, which is especially colorful in the wine regions.

In April you can see some of Spain's most spectacular fiestas, particularly Semana Santa (Holy Week); and by then the weather in southern Spain is warm enough to make sightseeing comfortable.

Spain is the number-one destination for European travelers; **to avoid crowds, come before June or after September.** Spaniards themselves vacation in August, and their annual migration to the

Your checklist for a perfect journey

WAY AHEAD
- Devise a trip budget.
- Write down the five things you want most from this trip. Keep this list handy before and during your trip.
- Make plane or train reservations. Book lodging and rental cars.
- Arrange for pet care.
- Check your passport. Apply for a new one if necessary.
- Photocopy important documents and store in a safe place.

A MONTH BEFORE
- Make restaurant reservations and buy theater and concert tickets. Visit fodors.com for links to local events.
- Familiarize yourself with the local language or lingo.

TWO WEEKS BEFORE
- Replenish your supply of medications.
- Create your itinerary.
- Enjoy a book or movie set in your destination to get you in the mood.

- Develop a packing list. Shop for missing essentials. Repair and launder or dry-clean your clothes.

A WEEK BEFORE
- Stop newspaper deliveries. Pay bills.
- Acquire traveler's checks.
- Stock up on film.
- Label your luggage.
- Finalize your packing list—take less than you think you need.
- Create a toiletries kit filled with travel-size essentials.
- Get lots of sleep. Don't get sick before your trip.

A DAY BEFORE
- Drink plenty of water.
- Check your travel documents.
- Get packing!

DURING YOUR TRIP
- Keep a journal/scrapbook.
- Spend time with locals.
- Take time to explore. Don't plan too much.

beach causes huge traffic jams on August 1 and 31. Major cities are relaxed and empty for the duration; small shops and some restaurants shut down for the entire month, but museums remain open.

CLIMATE

Summers in Spain are hot: temperatures frequently hit 100°F(38°C), and air-conditioning is not widespread. Try to **limit summer sightseeing to the morning hours.** That said, warm summer nights are among Spain's quiet pleasures.

Winters in Spain are mild and rainy along the coasts. Elsewhere, winter blows bitterly cold. Snow is infrequent except in the mountains, where you can ski from December to March in the Pyrenees and other resorts near Madrid.

➤ FORECASTS: **Weather Channel Connection** (tel. 900/932–8437 in the U.S.), 95¢ per minute.

The following are average daily maximum and minimum temperatures.

MADRID

Jan.	48F	9C	May	70F	21C	Sept.	77F	25C
	36	2		50	10		57	14
Feb.	52F	11C	June	81F	27C	Oct.	66F	19C
	36	2		59	15		50	10
Mar.	59F	15C	July	88F	31C	Nov.	55F	13C
	41	5		63	17		41	5
Apr.	64F	18C	Aug.	86F	30C	Dec.	48F	9C
	45	7		63	17		36	2

138

WORDS AND PHRASES

Basics

ENGLISH	SPANISH	PRONUNCIATION
Yes/no	Sí/no	see/no
Please	Por favor	pohr fah-vohr
May I?	¿Me permite?	meh pehr-mee-teh
Thank you (very much)	(Muchas) gracias	(moo-chas) grah-see-as
You're welcome	De nada	deh nah-dah
Excuse me	Con permiso/ perdón	con pehr-mee-so/ pehr-dohn
Pardon me/ what did you say?	¿Perdón?/Mande?	pehr-dohn/mahn-deh
Could you tell me . . . ?	¿Podría decirme . . . ?	po-dree-ah deh-seer-meh
I'm sorry	Lo siento	lo see-en-to
Good morning!	¡Buenos días!	bway-nohs dee-ahs
Good afternoon!	¡Buenas tardes!	bway-nahs tar-dess
Good evening!	¡Buenas noches!	bway-nahs no-chess
Goodbye!	¡Adiós!/ ¡Hasta luego!	ah-dee-ohss/ ah-stah-lwe-go
Mr./Mrs.	Señor/Señora	sen-yor/sen-yohr-ah
Miss	Señorita	sen-yo-ree-tah
Pleased to meet you	Mucho gusto	moo-cho goose-to
How are you?	¿Cómo está usted?	ko-mo es-tah oo-sted
Very well, thank you.	Muy bien, gracias.	moo-ee bee-en, grah-see-as
And you?	¿Y usted?	ee oos-ted
Hello (on the phone)	Diga	dee-gah

Numbers

1	un, uno	oon, oo-no
2	dos	dohs

3	tres	tress
4	cuatro	kwah-tro
5	cinco	sink-oh
6	seis	saice
7	siete	see-et-eh
8	ocho	o-cho
9	nueve	new-eh-veh
10	diez	dee-es
11	once	ohn-seh
12	doce	doh-seh
13	trece	treh-seh
14	catorce	ka-tohr-seh
15	quince	keen-seh
16	dieciséis	dee-es-ee-saice
17	diecisiete	dee-es-ee-see-et-eh
18	dieciocho	dee-es-ee-o-cho
19	diecinueve	dee-es-ee-new-ev-eh
20	veinte	vain-teh
21	veinte y uno/ veintiuno	vain-te-oo-noh
30	treinta	train-tah
32	treinta y dos	train-tay-dohs
40	cuarenta	kwah-ren-tah
50	cincuenta	seen-kwen-tah
60	sesenta	sess-en-tah
70	setenta	set-en-tah
80	ochenta	oh-chen-tah
90	noventa	no-ven-tah
100	cien	see-en
200	doscientos	doh-see-en-tohss
500	quinientos	keen-yen-tohss
1,000	mil	meel
2,000	dos mil	dohs meel

Days of the Week

Sunday	domingo	doh-meen-goh
Monday	lunes	loo-ness
Tuesday	martes	mahr-tess
Wednesday	miércoles	me-air-koh-less
Thursday	jueves	hoo-ev-ess
Friday	viernes	vee-air-ness
Saturday	sábado	sah-bah-doh

Useful Phrases

Do you speak English?	¿Habla usted inglés?	ah-blah oos-ted in-glehs
I don't speak Spanish	No hablo español	no ah-bloh es-pahn-yol
I don't understand (you)	No entiendo	no en-tee-en-doh
I understand (you)	Entiendo	en-tee-en-doh
I don't know	No sé	no seh
I am American/ British	Soy americano (americana)/ inglés(a)	soy ah-meh-ree-kah-no (ah-meh-ree-kah-nah)/in-glehs(ah)
My name is . . .	Me llamo . . .	meh yah-moh
Yes, please/ No, thank you	Sí, por favor/ No, gracias	see pohr fah-vor/ no grah-see-ahs
Yesterday/today/ tomorrow	Ayer/hoy/mañana	ah-yehr/oy/mahn-yah-nah
This morning/ afternoon	Esta mañana/tarde	es-tah mahn-yah-nah/tar-deh
Tonight	Esta noche	es-tah no-cheh
This/Next week	Esta semana/ la semana que entra	es-tah seh-mah-nah/lah seh-mah-nah keh en-trah
This/Next month	Este mes/el próximo mes	es-teh mehs/el prok-see-moh mehs
How?	¿Cómo?	koh-mo
When?	¿Cuándo?	kwahn-doh

What?	¿Qué?	keh
What is this?	¿Qué es esto?	keh es es-toh
Why?	¿Por qué?	por keh
Who?	¿Quién?	kee-yen
Where is . . . ?	¿Dónde está . . . ?	dohn-deh es-tah
the train station?	la estación del tren?	la es-tah-see-on del train
the subway station?	la estación del metro?	la es-ta-see-on del meh-tro
the bus stop?	la parada del autobus?	la pah-rah-dah del oh-toh-boos
the bank?	el banco?	el bahn-koh
the hotel?	el hotel?	el oh-tel
the post office?	la oficina de correos?	la oh-fee-see-nah deh-koh-reh-os
the museum?	el museo?	el moo-seh-oh
the hospital?	el hospital?	el ohss-pee-tal
the bathroom?	el baño?	el bahn-yoh
Here/there	Aquí/allá	ah-key/ah-yah
Open/closed	Abierto/cerrado	ah-bee-er-toh/ ser-ah-doh
Left/right	Izquierda/derecha	iss-key-er-dah/ dare-eh-chah
Straight ahead	Todo recto	toh-doh-rec-toh
Is it near/far?	¿Está cerca/lejos?	es-tah sehr-kah/ leh-hoss
I'd like . . .	Quisiera . . .	kee-see-ehr-ah
a room	una habitación	oo-nah ah-bee-tah-see-on
the key	la llave	lah yah-veh
a newspaper	un periódico	oon pehr-ee-oh-dee-koh
a stamp	un sello	say-oh
How much is this?	¿Cuánto cuesta?	kwahn-toh kwes-tah
A little/a lot	Un poquito/ mucho	oon poh-kee-toh/ moo-choh
More/less	Más/menos	mahss/men-ohss

I am ill	Estoy enfermo(a)	es-toy en-fehr-moh(mah)
Please call a doctor	Por favor llame un medico	pohr fah-vor ya-meh oon med-ee-koh
Help!	¡Ayuda!	ah-yoo-dah

On the Road

Avenue	Avenida	ah-ven-ee-dah
Broad, tree-lined boulevard	Paseo	pah-seh-oh
Highway	Carretera	car-reh-ter-ah
Port; mountain pass	Puerto	poo-ehr-toh
Street	Calle	cah-yeh
Waterfront promenade	Paseo marítimo	pah-seh-oh mahr-ee-tee-moh

In Town

Cathedral	Catedral	cah-teh-dral
Church	Iglesia	tem-plo/ee-glehs-see-ah
City hall, town hall	Ayuntamiento	ah-yoon-tah-me-yen-toh
Door, gate	Puerta	poo-ehr-tah
Main square	Plaza Mayor	plah-thah mah-yohr
Market	Mercado	mer-kah-doh
Neighborhood	Barrio	bahr-ree-o
Tavern, rustic restaurant	Mesón	meh-sohn
Traffic circle, roundabout	Glorieta	glor-ee-eh-tah
Wine cellar, wine bar, wine shop	Bodega	boh-deh-gah

Dining Out

| A bottle of . . . | Una bottella de . . . | oo-nah bo-teh-yah deh |
| A glass of . . . | Un vaso de . . . | oon vah-so deh |

Bill/check	La cuenta	lah kwen-tah
Breakfast	El desayuno	el deh-sah-yoon-oh
Dinner	La cena	lah seh-nah
Menu of the day	Menú del día	meh-noo del dee-ah
Fork	El tenedor	ehl ten-eh-dor
Is the tip included?	¿Está incluida la propina?	es-tah in-cloo-ee-dah lah pro-pee-nah
Knife	El cuchillo	el koo-chee-yo
Large portion of tapas	Ración	rah-see-ohn
Lunch	La comida	lah koh-mee-dah
Menu	La carta, el menú	lah cart-ah, el meh-noo
Napkin	La servilleta	lah sehr-vee-yet-ah
Please give me . . .	Por favor déme . . .	pohr fah-vor deh-meh
Spoon	Una cuchara	oo-nah koo-chah-rah

INDEX

FODOR'S POCKET MADRID 2001

EDITORS: Christine Cipriani, Laura M. Kidder

EDITORIAL CONTRIBUTOR: Edward Owen

Editorial Production: Marina Padakis

Maps: David Lindroth, *cartographer*; Bob Blake and Rebecca Baer, *map editors*

Design: Fabrizio La Rocca, *creative director*; Tigist Getachew, *art director*; Jolie Novak, *senior picture editor*; Melanie Marin, *photo editor*

Production/Manufacturing: Angela L. McLean

Cover Photograph: Ricardo Ordoñez/ Age Fotostock America

IMPORTANT TIP

Although all prices, opening times, and other details in this book are based on information supplied to us at press time, changes occur all the time in the travel world, and Fodor's cannot accept responsibility for facts that become outdated or for inadvertent errors or omissions. So **always confirm information when it matters,** especially if you're making a detour to visit a specific place.

SPECIAL SALES

Fodor's Travel Publications are available at special discounts for bulk purchases for sales promotions or premiums. Special editions, including personalized covers, excerpts of existing guides, and corporate imprints, can be created in large quantities for special needs. For more information, contact your local bookseller or write to Special Markets, Fodor's Travel Publications, 280 Park Avenue, New York, NY 10017. Inquiries from Canada should be directed to your local Canadian bookseller or sent to Random House of Canada, Ltd., Marketing Department, 2775 Matheson Boulevard East, Mississauga, Ontario L4W 4P7. Inquiries from the United Kingdom should be sent to Fodor's Travel Publications, 20 Vauxhall Bridge Road, London SW1V 2SA, England.

PRINTED IN THE UNITED STATES OF AMERICA

10 9 8 7 6 5 4 3 2 1